Praise For This Book

"With tender hands, a clear mind and an encouraging heart, Cali beautifully invites you to take hold of your most cherished dreams and move forward with them to create the life you know you can have."

Nick Williams author of *The Work We Were Born To Do* and co-founder of www.inspired-entrepreneur.com

"Don't Give Up Your Day Job *is a compelling read for anybody who wants to transform their life whilst still working part or full time. Cali Bird is a living testimony of somebody who has transformed her life from within the working world. So many coaching books are formidable because they encourage people to make radical changes or quantum leaps in their lives. Often these steps can appear daunting or over ambitious. This book provides a rich collection of case studies and clever insights from the author's own journey of success. Learning to tackle your inner gremlins with brilliance and fun makes this book unique in my opinion."*

Chris Smith

London Magazine 'A' List Coaches
Daily Telegraph's Top 20 Health Gurus
London Evening Standard's 50 Most Wanted Health Gurus

"If you're considering becoming your own boss, my view is that starting out whilst holding down the day job is the best way to start as you give yourself time to build confidence and cash. Any book that promotes the idea of part-time entrepreneurship has to be a good thing!"

Emma Jones founder of Enterprise Nation and author of
Working 5 to 0 how to start a successful business in your spare time

Don't Give Up Your Day Job

Practical ways to lead a fulfilling life and still pay the mortgage

Cali Bird

Matador
5 Weir Road
Kibworth Beauchamp
Leicester LE8 0LQ, UK
Tel: (+44) 116 279 2299
Fax: (+44) 116 279 2277
Email: books@troubador.co.uk
Web: www.troubador.co.uk/matador

ISBN 978 1848765 368

British Library Cataloguing in Publication Data.
A catalogue record for this book is available from the British Library.

Typeset in 11pt Garamond by Troubador Publishing Ltd, Leicester, UK
Printed and bound in the UK by TJ International Ltd, Padstow, Cornwall

Matador is an imprint of Troubador Publishing Ltd

Acknowledgements

A book does not happen on its own! I would like to thank all the fantastic people who have supported me through this process.

Firstly my book coach Mindy Gibbins-Klein (aka The Book Midwife) who helped me develop the theme and structure of the book and then applied just the right amount of pressure at regular intervals until the first draft of the manuscript was complete. A couple of drafts later the book was read by Beverley Bramwell, Anna Carvisiglia, Haseena Hassan, Barry Rice and Chris Smith. Thank you all for the time you spent going through the manuscript and for giving such useful feedback.

I would like to thank my family, my wonderful boyfriend, Graham, and my best friend, Helen, for supporting me in everything that I do. I also want to say a big thank you to the SGI Buddhists in Kennington who, over the years, have helped me to build a happy and jolly life.

Thank you to my mentors: Daisaku Ikeda for being such a great teacher in life and Nick Williams for all the inspiring talks over many years. You have both given me the knowledge and motivation to be the best person that I can be and to fulfil my mission.

I would also like to acknowledge and thank the late Graham Knight who allowed me to work a three day week, leaving me time for other pursuits. Additionally I would like to thank my colleagues in those IT departments for putting up with me not being at work on Thursdays and Fridays!

Thank you to the Pauls and staff at Sugarfree Design for coming up with such a fabulous cover and to all the folk at Matador for making my dream of being a published author finally come true.

Nam-myoho-renge-kyo. Thank you.

Table Of Contents

Introduction

Thank you very much for buying or borrowing this book. My aim is to convince you that hope and fulfilment are possible even if you hate your day job or feel trapped by your current circumstances. My philosophy as a life coach is that you do not have to take the scary step of immediately quitting your occupation in order to achieve a happier life, but you do need to start taking action towards what you would rather be doing. This might be anything from resurrecting a hobby to starting to lay the groundwork for a career change or new business.

I know from my own experience that when you have 'plan B' bubbling along nicely on the side the day job is less painful. The knowledge that you are building an escape route lessens the stress of your current employment and makes it easier to stay in the job until you feel ready to leave. Spending time on a hobby or cause that you are passionate about will provide you with a comfort cushion which will absorb some of the stresses of your current responsibilities.

The book is organised into two parts. The first part is about discovering what you really want for your life and then building a realistic action plan towards it. Even if your dreams and goals seem impractical or 'pie in the sky' you will nevertheless uncover some easy and tangible steps which you can take right now. This will help you build momentum towards your goals and you might even begin to feel that your dream is within your grasp after all.

The second part is about overcoming blocks, procrastination

and obstacles such as the lack of time and money. It will also teach you how to stop your head freaking out when your heart wants to follow its deepest desires! If you already know exactly what you want for your life and how to get there, but you are having trouble getting going then you can skip straight to part two. However I recommend that you still take the time to go back to part one at a later date.

Throughout the book you will find exercises for you to complete. You don't have to do them but you will get the most value from the book, not to mention some good ideas, if you do. Most of them are fairly quick and, depending on the exercise, there is space to jot your thoughts down straight away.

The most important thing to remember is that it doesn't matter how long it takes you to achieve your goals, or how many times you over-shoot any deadlines for them, but it does matter that you get started now on doing something towards them and continue to take action whenever you can. If I can inspire you to begin your journey to a happier and more fulfilled life then the mission of this book will be accomplished.

Now get reading, get started on your dreams and have fun!

part ONE

chapter 1:

You Don't Have To Give Up Your Day Job

It's not all or nothing

It is a myth that in order to lead a fulfilling and wholesome life you have to immediately give up your mundane, boring or stressful job – the job that you never intended to do anyway let alone for the last five, ten or fifteen years! It does not have to be true that in order to earn lots of money you have to do a job you hate and that doing a job you love will bring in less money. It is possible to earn sufficient money and enjoy your life at the same time.

My philosophy as a life coach is that you don't need to give up your day job tomorrow in order to achieve your dreams, but you do need to start taking action towards them *while* you still carry out your current responsibilities. I call this developing 'plan B' on the side. I have found from my own experience, and from that of my coaching clients, that developing your own 'plan B' outside of work reduces stress from within the workplace. If you are starting to take action towards your desired life then you are no longer trapped by your day job. You know that eventually there will be a life beyond it. Also, because you are being motivated to take action for yourself, some of that motivation and excitement will inevitably spill over into your day job and this

3

will make it easier and less stressful. It doesn't matter how long it takes to achieve your dreams, what matters is that you start to do something towards them and continue with this action when you can.

Before we get into the nitty-gritty I would like to share my own story with you, to show you that it took me fourteen years from the time I first decided that I wanted to be a motivational speaker to when I gave my first personal development seminar for money under the banner of *Lead The Life You Want To Lead*.

For my first job I ended up training to be a chartered accountant at a prestigious firm of accountants in London. This was not something I had planned to do. At university I had studied music but as I neared the end of my degree I realised that the only music related careers open to me were being a music teacher or an unemployed flute player. Neither of these appealed so I trotted off to the university careers service where they advised me to go into accountancy. They claimed that I didn't need a relevant degree, it would give me a solid business background and I would triple my salary in three years. They were right. The business knowledge to this day is extremely useful and I did ratchet myself up the salary food-chain in a short amount of time. As soon as I qualified I left the world of debits and credits and went into investment banking. It was a lot sexier than being an auditor but it wasn't the life that I had dreamed of and it did not honour my creative abilities.

During my mid-twenties I went backpacking through South-East Asia and finally arrived in Sydney where I intended to work for a few months. While I was there I came across Herbalife, a nutrition and weight-loss company, that worked on a multi-level marketing basis. (Don't panic, this book isn't about pyramid selling or flogging stuff to your friends!) Herbalife introduced me into

4

the world of motivational speakers. I attended their conferences and seminars and was transfixed by the wisdom, panache and knowledge of the people who led them, particularly the late Jim Rohn. (For those of you that have never heard of Jim Rohn, he was one of Anthony Robbins's teachers. Apparently the young Anthony used to be on the door collecting the admission fee for some of Jim's seminars. In recent years Jim has become known as the grand-daddy of the personal development world.) During these talks I realised that I didn't care that much about selling weight loss products but that I did want to be the person up on the podium, giving the talk and inspiring an audience. The seeds of *Lead The Life You Want To Lead* had been planted.

When I returned to the UK I went back into investment banking and gradually moved from a finance to a technology role and eventually I became an IT consultant. In 1999 I was fortunate to be earning what I called "more money than God" but I was thoroughly bored and unfulfilled. However, during that year three important events occurred.

Firstly, I saw Jim Rohn speak in London and I remembered that I had this dream to be a motivational speaker. However now the dream troubled me. I had observed that speakers such as Jim Rohn had a story that went something like "once I was broke then I met a teacher who taught me stuff that made me rich and now I'm going to make even more money teaching you the same stuff". They had achieved an extraordinary transition in their lives and then sold the story of how they had done it. Unfortunately for me I lacked the *after* picture: I had the *before* picture of "once upon a time I was an accountant and a computer programmer" but could not say "and now I do this and it's fabulous and I'm going to teach you how you too can be as fabulous as me"!

5

The second significant event of 1999 initially looked as though it could have been a solution to my problem. I was on holiday and decided, for fun, to see an astrologer. I explained my predicament that I felt I had so much more potential but I didn't have a clue how to tap that potential. He too had a creative background in classical music and had worked in IT. He suggested that I start writing a journal, do it for a year and see what came out of it. Then he looked at my astrology chart, said lots of things that went over my head and then exclaimed, "You have Gemini in your mid heaven [or something like that]; this suggests you'd be very good at writing."

For me this was a light bulb moment. The only job I had ever enjoyed from my IT experience was when I worked as a trainer and wrote the training manuals. I had found it satisfying, tangible and, despite being about human resource systems, it had an element of creativity about it. The astrologer recommended two books for me to work through, both were by Julia Cameron: *The Right To Write* and *The Artist's Way*. I went straight to the bookshop, bought the books and a journal, and started there and then.

I was very excited about my writing because I thought it would give me the solution to my problem. Now I would be able to say in talks "once upon a time I was an accountant and a computer programmer, now I'm a bestselling author and this is how I did it". Hurrah! I had my *after* picture but unfortunately I realised that becoming a bestselling author is not a quick or easy endeavour – more on that later!

The third significant event of 1999 happened a few weeks after my New York trip: I came across a British inspirational speaker called Nick Williams. Over the next three years I went to many of Nick's talks, workshops and seminars. I was also writing the early drafts of a novel and had managed to persuade my IT client to let me work part-time instead of full-time so that I had more time to write.

I have practiced Buddhism since 1988 and regularly give study lectures within our Buddhist movement. In late 2002 I gave a lecture about the Buddhist perspective of mission and life purpose. The lectures are given on a voluntary basis and are nothing to do with business. However I received exceptionally good feedback from members of the audience on that particular lecture and I started to wonder if the time had arrived for me to speak professionally, on secular themes, in the outside world. I also noticed that although I was not yet a published author, I was inspiring the people around me with my creative efforts. At work, other writers came out of the woodwork and were impressed that I used to write every morning before going to the office. With Nick's encouragement I decided to give a one-off prototype motivational talk to family, friends and friends of friends. I gave this talk on 16th October 2003 in a function room at my local pub to an audience of over twenty people. *Lead The Life You Want To Lead* had been born.

At that time I didn't take the talk any further but kept working away on my writing and working part-time in IT. At the beginning of 2005 I was informed that my long-running IT contract was going to be terminated. At first I panicked but then I decided to make this the springboard for advancement and, on Wednesday 30th March 2005, made the declaration that I had no idea how I was going to achieve it but I *was* going to be a professional speaker. That summer I trained to be a life coach, resurrected my *Lead The Life You Want To Lead* ideas and started to build a personal development practice. The following year on 25th November 2006 I gave that first paid-for workshop.

7

Since then I have still done bits and pieces of IT work, I give personal development talks, I run workshops, I coach people, I do corporate training on a personal development theme and I speak at various Mind Body Soul events. All of this gives me more than a sufficient income and I am leading the life I want to lead.

Back to the novel, which isn't a bestseller yet! I have sent it off it off to numerous literary agents all of whom politely turned it down. I have written a further five drafts of it, each one an improvement on the one before and despatched those to the publishing industry too – so far to no avail. I have also taken creative writing courses though they haven't yet transformed my fiction writing ability into Booker prize winning potential! As I said earlier, it doesn't matter how long it takes you to achieve your dreams or succeed with your goals, what matters is that you get started and keep going. I will continue to persist with that particular dream.

I wanted to tell you my own story with its successes and 'not yet successes' because I want you to be assured that there is nothing that I am writing about in this book that I haven't experienced or done myself. If I can gradually win with my goals, no matter how impossible they sometimes seem, then I know that you can too.

Don't quit your job tomorrow

Sometimes when we are unhappy with our life, perhaps on a day when the commute to work is spectacularly awful and we get home from work so late that we are barely inclined to eat dinner let alone do anything else, it is tempting to think that quitting our job would be the answer to all our problems. If it weren't for the job you would be happy. If only you had only got around to starting that fabulous business idea you had ten years ago then everything would be all right now. If only you had persisted with those guitar lessons then you might have been a famous rock star and have a cushy and well paid job as a judge on *X Factor*. If only you had summoned up the courage to stick with your art degree all those years ago then you might have been mates with Damien Hirst and Tracey Emin. You cannot change the past but you can change the way you feel about the future.

When you have a seed of desire to follow an alternative or dream occupation it is common to think that you need to do this to the exclusion of your day job; all of the dream or none of it. You might be girding your loins to march into the boss's office tomorrow, hand in your resignation and exchange your laptop and your Blackberry for a P45 and a pass to freedom. You might feel that it is a now or never moment. You might feel ready to take on the challenge of your own business, your own creativity or a career change to a more rewarding occupation.

But quitting your job is a scary move. How will you pay the mortgage, school fees or keep your car on the road? How will you explain this sudden manoeuvre to your spouse, or your best friend or your parents? What if the grand plan doesn't work out or doesn't pull in sufficient cash before your savings evaporate? What if it turns out that you are crap at business, or writing or making music? What if you get that job working for a worthwhile charity and discover that not only does it suck just as much as your current job but it only pays half as much?

So you don't quit. You resentfully stay in your job, you humour your boss and your colleagues; and another ten years go by.

That's why I say: don't give up your day job. It is too much pressure to put on yourself and on your business, creative or occupational ideas. The chances of succeeding are too low. Sure, some people make it work but most don't. It can also take longer than you think to get a new endeavour to a sufficiently profitable state. If you do chuck the job and then get badly burned you may get put off trying again at some point in the future. Then your dreams will be buried under more fear and hurt than they are right now. A job provides other benefits in addition to a pay cheque for which they are not often given credit. Your job gives you routine, purpose, comradeship, status, achievement and someone with whom you can dissect the current revelations from your favourite soap opera. Very often you don't realise those benefits exist until you no longer have them.

Keep your job security and find other ways to be fulfilled

If you are going to stick with the day job, at least for the time being, then what are the other ways in which you can find fulfilment? Below you will find some ideas that may work for you.

Work Part-Time

Take a leaf out of my book and work part-time. If you are a valuable asset to your current employer then they may be willing to let you cut down to three or four days a week. There are many benefits for your employer with this arrangement. For a start, they get to keep your knowledge and skill set. You are also likely to be more motivated because it is in your interest to make the arrangement work. Finally, I believe that part-time staff are more productive because they have less opportunity to catch up on work if time is wasted on surfing the internet, taking a long lunch or doing nothing on a Friday afternoon; so they don't behave like this as much as full-time employees might. Part-time staff are also motivated to ensure that work is completed or loose ends tied up so that problems do not occur on the days that they are not at work.

I have worked part-time several times in my career and I can honestly say it is the best of both worlds. I have earned enough money to cover my bills and I have had the time to develop my creative interests and pursue my dream of building a personal development business. As time has gone on I have even come to enjoy my IT work. It satisfies the nerdy side of my brain and I enjoy the comradeship and teamwork that comes with it.

Working part-time allows a gradual transition to a new life. You keep the security and familiarity of the old while developing the skills and knowledge you will need for the future. Your colleagues are a wonderful network of people who know, trust and like you and you may find that they become your first customers in your new endeavour. Similarly, your current employer might become your first client. If you are still present in their world then they will be interested in how your 'plan B on the side' is going and what they can do to help you with it. If you leave the company then you fade from their consciousness and the connections you built up slowly become out of date.

Find another way to scratch that itch
Another way of having the best of both worlds is to find an alternative way to satisfy your unfulfilled urges. For example, suppose you work as a lawyer but you have always had a desire to

teach. It would be very daunting to walk away from such a well paid occupation but there may be other ways to experience teaching while still keeping the security of your current pay cheque. Maybe there is a scheme at your workplace which mentors local school children. This would be fantastic because then you can get a flavour of life with children in school.

You might find that this satisfies your urge to teach and you can continue in your job as well as participate in the programme. Alternatively you might find that you love the mentoring work so much and this confirms to you that you really do want to be a teacher which may then make it easier to make the jump and start the training. Finally you may discover that you hate the school environment and you never want to teach in a million years – this is a fantastic realisation because you still have your lawyer's job and you haven't done anything stupid like walking away from it. In fact, if this latter case were true you might even begin to enjoy your job a little more and find other advantages in staying put!

Ian always wanted to be a journalist when he was younger but ended up training to be an engineer. He felt that at the age of forty-five it just wasn't realistic to give up his engineering career and take his chances as a rooky reporter and he found himself full of regret and deep-seated anger that he didn't try out as a journalist twenty years ago. In order to get through this pain he decided to find ways to play at being a journalist within his existing career. He got involved with the company newsletter and also began to submit articles to the engineering trade press. As a qualified engineer with a flair for writing this turned out to be a winning formula and he now gets a quite few pieces published but he doesn't have to worry about making a living from his writing.

Hobbies

Sometimes, overcoming dissatisfaction with your life may be as simple as developing a new hobby, or resurrecting an old one. When I coached Mary she told me that she was fed-up with her job and lifestyle but she didn't know what she wanted to do instead. I asked her what she was passionate about. After a brief hesitation on her part the conversation went something like this:

"Well I think the environment is important, and I used to like going wind-surfing and I love cooking."

"Brilliant," I replied, "when did you last wind-surf or throw a dinner party?"

"I don't know," said Mary. "I never cook properly these days and I haven't been out on a lake in years."

"Would you like to do one of these things in the next couple of weeks?" I asked.

"Sure," she replied.

And then we discussed the logistics of how she could get herself back on water. When I spoke to her a week later she had booked a surfing lesson and was busy co-ordinating a group of friends to come over at the weekend for dinner.

You don't necessarily have to do anything deeply profound, meaningful or scary to feel happy with your life. Sometimes it is as simple as making the commitment to spend a couple of hours doing something you really enjoy once a week, once a fortnight or once a month.

Don't wait until you are retired to have the life you want

It is tempting to give up on having the life you want while you are still of working age and wait until retirement to have a more enjoyable lifestyle or explore creative pursuits. However, that's a long time to be miserable. Such misery and the related stress that goes with it can cause other problems such as illness, depression or the breakdown of a relationship. Life can become a continual downward spiral.

Speaking of illness, what if you don't live until retirement age? Then you will have missed out on the opportunity to lead the life you want. I was galvanised in my thirties firstly to find the time to write and then a few years later to begin my personal development business because two of my friends, also in their thirties, suffered from cancer. Thankfully both of them survived and are fit and healthy today. Their illnesses really brought home to me the need to shoot for my dreams there and then, rather than keep tolerating a professional life which wasn't making me happy and risk never getting the opportunity to work towards my heart's desire.

It is very easy to fall into 'when/then' syndrome. When I have the perfect job, then I'll be happy. When I have a husband, then I'll feel complete. When I earn £50,000 a year, then I'll start investing in my future. Again, with this approach to life happiness is postponed to a later date. You risk never getting the thing which you believe will give you contentment, or worse than that, you get it but then discover that you still don't feel any better.

'When/then' syndrome also causes you to continually obsess about what you don't have. The irony of this is that you can end up driving away the very object you desire. Although I was fortunate in building a more fulfilling work and creative life in my thirties, the one thing I lacked which I really really wanted was a boyfriend; someone of husband potential with whom I could have a long lasting relationship and possibly a family. One by one my friends paired up and got married but I was still living a Bridget Jones existence and this caused me a lot of pain. I would frequently feel depressed, be at a loss with myself and obsess about ways to meet men and why I couldn't seem to attract any decent ones. On the rare occasions when I did get to go out on a date I'm sure they could smell my desperation to get married and have children because a second date never seemed to be forthcoming. Eventually after building wisdom from my Buddhist practice, digging deep based on my personal development journey and some counselling sessions, I realised that I had to be happy as I was. It dawned on me that if a fairy godmother arrived and gave me a cast iron guarantee that Mr Right would pitch up in exactly twelve months time, I wouldn't spend that twelve months moping about because I didn't have a bloke. Safe in the knowledge that he was on the way I would get out, enjoy life and do the things I love to do. When I decided to live with that spirit, hey presto, in the nick of time before I turned forty, a wonderful man came into my life and I am going to marry him next year.

This is why I urge you to find ways to live some of your dream life now. You don't know what's around the corner and you don't know whether the next financial crash will swipe away your pension pot just when you were ready to start enjoying it. Just like deciding when to have children, there is probably never a perfect time when the conditions are exactly right, when you have enough money and when all around you are in full agreement with your plans. So you might as well start now and stop waiting for that golden tomorrow.

Exercise

What are you passionate about? What hobbies did you used to enjoy? What new activity would you love to try? Think of ten ways in which you could get a taster of your dream job or lifestyle and decide which one of these you would like to act on this week.

1._____

2._____

3._____

4._____

5._____

6._____

7._____

8._____

9._____

10._____

You don't have to walk away from your job or your family, you just have to start taking one or two steps in a new or different direction. Remember, it doesn't matter how long it takes you to achieve your dream life or succeed in your goals, what matters is that you start doing something about them and continue to take action whenever you can. Imagine leading the life of your dreams and knowing that you are in control of your journey towards them. Doesn't this make you feel better? If you could find just a couple of things to do which help you to conjure up this feeling, then isn't it worth doing them?

chapter 2:

What Does Your Dream Look Like?

It is easier to start taking action towards a better life if you know what you actually want. However, some people have no idea what they want and get quite frustrated when asked this question. If you are one of these people and you already feel like chucking this book into the bin along with the other personal development books which told you to "clearly define your goals" then fear not – jump straight to the section called *What Don't You Want?* on page 20. There you will find an alternative way of helping you define what you would like for your future. For everyone else, read on!

What do you want?

There are many words that can be used to define your future. You may be thinking about making your dreams come true, or having a list of goals and achieving them, or satisfying your aspirations, or having strong desires or maybe you want an ideal life. This book will use the words goal, dream, ideal life, aspirations and desires interchangeably – you know which one appeals to you most and you will have your own thoughts about what that word means to you. Irrespective of how I lexicographically dress it up, what I'm really asking you is "What do you want for your life?"

- Maybe you want to undertake creative pursuits and publish your first book.
- Maybe you want to play lead guitar in a band and do gigs at the weekend.
- Maybe you want to act in or produce your own film.
- Maybe you want to drive a Porsche or a classic car.
- Maybe you want to be fitter and healthier – and weigh two stone less than you do now.
- Maybe you want to learn how to dance the Argentinean Tango the Cha-Cha or the Viennese Waltz.
- Maybe you want to grow your own vegetables or keep chickens.
- Maybe you want a husband or a wife or a significant other. Or maybe you want to be free of the one you already have.
- Maybe you want to run your own business. Maybe that business must fit around the demands of raising a child.
- Maybe you would like to move from the city to a small holding in the country.
- Maybe you want to have a roof-top apiary on your city-centre apartment.
- Maybe you want to own a string of properties and earn enough from the rents so that you don't need a regular job.
- Maybe you aspire to being a senior manager, a director or CEO, but first you'll have to get an MBA.
- Maybe you want to earn a six figure salary, or pocket a seven figure bonus.
- Maybe you want a major career change.

- Maybe you want to go to university and study archaeology or French literature.

Maybe you don't have a clue what you see yourself doing in the future but you would love to own a house with a conservatory that looks out on a beautiful garden.

Exercise

Imagine yourself in five years time. What are the details of your life at that time? Where will you be living – and with whom? What work or combination of work will you be doing? What leisure activities will you be enjoying? What will you know then that you don't know now? What will be your greatest achievement between now and then?

If five years ahead seems an impossibly long time into the future then just imagine the next one or two years.

What don't you want?

In this segment we will build a vision for your future based upon what you don't like about your current life. If you have no idea what you would like for your future and / or you drew a blank in the last exercise then you may find this approach easier. If you found the last exercise easy and you have a clear plan for your future then feel free to jump ahead to the next section which starts on page 26.

I'm guessing that you were attracted to this book because there is something about your life with which you are not happy. It may be that you are unhappy with just one or two factors or perhaps you feel trapped and fed up about everything.

Alternatively, maybe life isn't too bad at the moment but you feel that you are lacking in clarity or direction for the future.

In the exercise below we are going to identify what is causing you pain at the moment and then use this information to build a picture of what you may want in the future. For example, Gerry hates the fact that he works long hours and this was compounded by his commute which takes over an hour each way. In the future Gerry needs a job closer to home and/or in an organisation that promotes better work/life balance. Allison is driven mad by her domestic circumstances. Her house is too far from the train station and getting the bus to the station adds a tedious extra piece to her commute. In the future she wants to live somewhere which is only five or ten minutes walk to the best transport links. Nigel is sick of fighting with his flatmates for the bathroom, particularly with Lucy who spends hours in there and then leaves wet towels all over the floor. He wants to start planning on finding a way to live on his own. Failing that, he wants to live with just one other person who takes very quick showers!

Exercise

Write down what dissatisfies you, what you hate or what drives you mad about each of the areas of life listed below. Then come up with two realistic solutions and two completely unrealistic, yet fun and fulfilling, alternatives. Really go to town on the unrealistic ideas as you might as well enjoy dreaming about them.

For example:

Don't like: the fact that my boss always expects me to be available for phone calls at the weekend.

Realistic solutions:

1. Give her some times when it is OK to phone and make it clear when it isn't appropriate.

2. Stop worrying about it. Just because she has no family or personal life doesn't mean that I have to feel guilty about wanting to make the most of mine.

Completely unrealistic yet fun and/or fulfilling alternatives:

1.   Accidentally drop my Blackberry into a bucket of water.

2.   Hand in my notice tomorrow and get a job as a scuba-diver.

Over to you:

Job / Work

Don't like _____

_____

_____

Realistic solutions:

1.

2.

Completely unrealistic yet fun and/or fulfilling alternatives:

1.

2.

Money / Wealth

Don't like _____

_____

_____

Realistic solutions:

1.

2.

Completely unrealistic yet fun and/or fulfilling alternatives:

1.

2.

Friends and Relationships

Don't like _____

_____

_____

Realistic solutions:

1.

2.

Completely unrealistic yet fun and/or fulfilling alternatives:

1.

2.

Home

Don't like _____

_____

_____

Realistic solutions:

1.

2.

Completely unrealistic yet fun and/or fulfilling alternatives:

1.

2.

Health

Don't like _____

_____

_____

Realistic solutions:

1.

2.

Completely unrealistic yet fun and/or fulfilling alternatives:

1.

2.

Spare time / Play / Fun

Don't like _____

_____

_____

Realistic solutions

1.

2.

I hope you had fun with this exercise. I wonder whether there were any common themes or re-occurrences in your dislikes and your proposed solutions. And I wonder if this exercise revealed one or two dreams or aspirations that you would love to experience at some point in the future. You never know, by the time you have finished reading this book, the unrealistic ideas might not seem so outlandish and impossible!

Hopefully as you continue reading you will get other ideas on how to address some of these areas of dissatisfaction. It would be such a shame if in five years time you were still begrudgingly working long hours in a job you hate, still being passed over for promotion or still struggling to earn enough money for your basic needs. If you are stuck in a dead-end job which you feel is going to be just as dull and poorly paid in five years time as it is now then perhaps you could think of six other ways to earn your crust. Even if five of these ideas turn out to be totally unrealistic, one of them might be worth thinking about.

Get your dream documented

Hopefully the content and exercises of the previous two sections will have helped you to pull together a vision for your future. For some of you this will be radically different from your current life, while for others, you just need to tweak one or two things.

However different your dream is from today's reality I recommend that you commit this dream, or your goals, to paper. Notice the use of the word *commit* in the last sentence. There is something about writing down your goals, or documenting them using pictures, that assists your commitment to achieving these goals. In documenting them you are making effort and doing something practical rather than just wishing for a better future without taking any action towards it. Something magic happens when you make this effort to write down your dreams. The universe begins to notice that you really are serious about achieving them and it might start to give you a helping hand. You find that synchronicity kicks in and you bump into someone you've never met before who just happens to be at your friend's birthday party and discover that this person can give you useful information or steer you in the right direction.

It is also extremely satisfying to come across a dream which you wrote down some time ago and realise that you have achieved it. When I returned from my back-packing trip to Australia I was very keen to finally own my own flat rather than go back to sharing a rented house with others. As part of an exercise suggested in a book I was reading by Jim Rohn, I wrote down a few paragraphs which described the property that I wanted to buy. Many years later, around the time when I started my coaching business, I was clearing out my home office and I found that piece of paper where I had written down my dream home. The description that I had written all those years earlier matched exactly the flat in which I was very happily living.

Some of you may be reluctant to document your dreams

because you feel an onus to achieve them and you are scared that you might fail. Some of the goals that I have achieved took much longer than I thought and I have suffered many setbacks and failures with them along the way. So I know the pain of failing in something that I really want, of picking myself up, trying again and still not making it. You reach a point where it is difficult to re-determine and try again. When you are in this state and someone breezily tells you to make a commitment in writing to your goals and aspirations, you might want to punch them instead!

I went through this recently with regards to my weight. Most of my life I have been very lucky in that I have been quite naturally thin. However, four years ago when I got together with my boyfriend I started to put on weight and very steadily piled on two and a half stone. I was no longer a slender and elegant gazelle and none of my clothes fitted. Instead I started to look middle-aged, my neck and face thickened out and my waist measurement was a few inches in excess of that recommended as healthy by the medical profession. I also hated buying clothes in a bigger size.

Every time I stood on the scales my old weight gradually disappeared from sight on the dial on the scales and it seemed impossible that I would ever be that weight again. In the end I decided to join Weight Watchers. The first thing you have to do with Weight Watchers is decide on your goal weight and write it down. As a coach I know all about writing down goals but I found this ever so hard because I did not feel confident that I could get back to my old weight and I was scared of committing to a goal and then having to endure the pain of failing to reach it. I read up on the Weight Watchers method and studied the testimonials on their website and saw that this was a tried and tested method. I realised that if I stuck to the method, went to the meetings every week to support my efforts then it just might work for me. Only then was I able to write down my goal weight. As I made that written commitment I felt exhilarated and ready to get started. I am pleased to report that in the last four months I have lost 19.5 pounds and have only 8.5 pounds left to lose in order to reach my target weight.

Knowing that I was plugging into a system that had proven successes of weight loss helped me to summon up my courage and go for it. In writing this book my aim is to provide you with a similar method; a system you can use to either change your life completely for the better, or make small changes to how you live so that you feel that your life contains some fulfilling activities.

Please find the courage to start this journey by documenting how you would like your life to be in the future. In the next section we'll discuss different ways to do this and you can choose the method or methods that most appeal to you. Remember that your written goals are personal to you. You don't have to show anyone else or even tell them that you are embarking on this journey.

Ways to document your future

Below I set out three ways that you can document your future dreams and goals. One or two of them will appeal to you and you may also want to have a play with a second method. It doesn't matter which one you choose, so long as you document something.

1. Write about your ideal life
This method is how I described my flat, all those years ago. I just

sat down and wrote about it. You don't have to re-create *War and Peace*, just two or three paragraphs will suffice (but you can write more than this if you wish). Write about where you would like to live in the future, the type of work you will be doing and/or the kind of lifestyle that you will have. You can write specifically about how much you will be earning, if you know that level of detail, or write more generally about what you will be able to afford. Put in as much or as little as you know and include other people who may be living this life with you. You can write beautifully crafted paragraphs, or in note form, or bullet points or a mixture of all of these. As you write this story of your future, enjoy painting a picture in words and evoking emotions of how wonderful this future life is going to feel.

2. Make a vision board

Making a vision board is a really fun exercise where you step back into the realms of playschool and you find pictures from magazines and newspapers that represent your future dreams. You will also need a large piece of card or paper (about A2 or A1 size) and a picture of yourself.

You can either take a trip to the stationery shop and buy a suitable sized piece of card or you can have fun improvising. Perhaps you have a roll of wallpaper lying around that you can cut a piece from and use the reverse side, or a sheet of flipchart paper will work. Failing that grab some sellotape and stick either four or six pieces of regular sized Letter or A4 paper together to form a larger sheet.

Take the photo of yourself and stick it with glue or sellotape in the middle of your sheet. Grab yourself a stack of old magazines and newspapers and then spend no longer than half an hour rifling through them and ripping out the images that appeal to you and evoke what you would like for your future. Stick these images around the picture of yourself on your vision board.

Additionally you can use the internet as a source of images. One of my goals is to have such a huge following that I need to use the Royal Albert Hall to do a talk, so I went on the internet and found a picture of the hall and placed it on my vision board.

You can also fake your dream using photographs. I once made a mock-up of my novel, went to the flagship store of a well-known book chain and had a friend take photos of me and my book in the bestsellers section. We also found a table and created a fake book signing. I tried to get a photo of myself in front of the logo of the bookstore but security had rumbled us by then and asked us to leave! Photoshop can also enable you to create wonderful pictures of your future. Have fun with this exercise and place the results on your vision board.

Many of the items on my vision board represent big long term goals and may take me some time to achieve. I have a section containing logos of media outlets or TV shows in which I would like to be featured. Some of these I have already succeeded with, others are still dreams. It is fun when you can start to tick off items as accomplished. If the goals on your vision board seem impossible or too long term then make sure you put a few easy things on there too, like a pair of fabulous shoes that you've spotted, or a piece of sports equipment that you can treat yourself to. Again, the internet can be very useful for finding pictures of these objects of desire.

You can also make your own pictures. Whether you are a talented artist or only capable of drawing stick people, have fun with sketching out some scenes that represent your dreams. Again, take yourself back to the time when you were a child and enjoy using coloured pens, pencils or paints to create your dream.

The whole point of making a vision board is that it is fun. Don't spend hours and hours making it perfect. Quickly find or make some images and stick them on. You can add to it over time or make a new one at some point in the future.

When your vision board is complete put it somewhere where you can look at it on a regular basis. Spend time in front of it focussing on your dreams and visualising them happening. If you live with other people and you want to keep your vision board private, then attach it to the inside of your wardrobe door. That way you can look at it every morning as you get dressed but it is not on display to anyone else.

3. Write a list of goals

Rather than creating expressive paragraphs or putting together a vision board, you may simply want to write a list of goals. Your list might be quite short, containing between five or ten goals, or you might want to write a long list of everything you would like to achieve in your future. Your list may feature realistic goals as well as some more outlandish desires.

Next to each item on your list, write a date by when you would like it to be achieved. You will find that some of the items will be achieved by the date specified and other items may take longer. It doesn't matter if your goals take longer than you originally thought, what matters is that you keep taking action towards them. It is better to set a magnificent goal and only achieve half of it than never dare to go for your dreams and live a life of regret. As they say, if you shoot for the moon then at worst, you will land among the stars.

If you don't achieve a goal by its original 'achieve by' date then change the date. Review what activities you need to undertake in order to complete it and also consider breaking the goal down into a series of smaller goals – that way you can have the satisfaction of ticking off each stage or the larger goal as complete. For example, I have wanted to be a published author for many years. My original goal of 'write a bestselling book' hasn't come true yet and I have parked my novel for the time being. However, in writing this book the goals have been more about the different stages of writing and publishing a book, for example: write down the overall themes, plan each chapter, start writing, complete the first ten thousand words, complete the first draft, edit the first draft, decide on publishing options, prepare the manuscript for publication, write the marketing plan for the book, begin executing the marketing task. This approach has made it much easier to measure and tick off my progress as each of these smaller goals were accomplished. Again, some of these goals took a little longer than expected but each time I was motivated to get back on track, get the task done and reach the next milestone.

Exercise

You've guessed it – if you haven't already done so then document your dream using one or two of the methods described above. Whichever one(s) you decide to go for, don't make it too much of a work of art – just get on and get it done quickly.

In the next couple of chapters we will seek out realistic and logistical ways to make a start on what you have just documented, even for the goals which feel as though they are 'pie in the sky'. You will soon have plenty of ideas of simple tasks that you can do right now, alongside your day job and current responsibilities that will set you on the road towards your new, improved life.

chapter 3:

What Do You Need To Gain?

What do you need to acquire to make your dreams come true?

Now that you have decided what you want for your future and have written it down using words or pictures, you may be wondering how on earth you are going to achieve these dreams. Panic not – the next three chapters are going to give you plenty of ideas for getting started on them. This chapter is about figuring out what you would need to gain in order to achieve the dreams and goals that you documented in the last section. For example, if you want to be operating at board level in your career in five years time then you might need to gain an MBA in the intervening period. If you want to become a teacher then you will need a teaching qualification. If you want to own a spa and wellness centre somewhere on the Mediterranean Sea then you will need to find the right property or a piece of land.

Some of what you need to gain may be of a simpler, everyday nature. If you want to get fit then you might need to gain a training buddy or a personal trainer. If you want to learn to play the piano you will need to gain a piano teacher and a piano, if you don't already have one.

34

If you want to get your business off the ground then you many need to gain an extra day a week to work on it. If you want to go horse-riding or sailing then you many need to gain a couple of hours at the weekend to do this.

Perhaps you need to gain some skills. To take your business to the next level you may need to gain some marketing or sales skills, or gain someone else who can do these activities for you. You may need to gain confidence in public speaking or some opportunities to give some talks so that you feel more comfortable at speaking in public. If you want to go travelling or live in foreign climes then you may need to learn a new language. If your dream is to have your own acupuncture practice then not only will you have to learn how to do acupuncture but you may also need to gain some general business skills. If you are an urbanite, who always uses public transport, and your dream is to live or work rurally then you will need to gain a car. If you can't drive then you will need to learn, hence you will need to gain a driving instructor as well as a willing volunteer with whom you can practise your driving.

You may also need to gain some intangibles. Very often when people come on my workshops or ask about coaching they say that they need to gain some clarity on which direction to take in the future. Perhaps you need to gain some self confidence or an injection of self belief. Maybe you need to build a higher level of self esteem, or become more comfortable at making friends or building relationships. All of these factors will bring you closer towards your goals and help you to navigate your way through the more logistical action points that you will need to take.

I have already said this at least once and I will no doubt say it a few more times before the end of the book: it doesn't matter how long it takes you to achieve your dreams. If some of the things you need to gain are huge or of a long term nature, so what? Now is as good a time as any to start working towards them. If you want to learn to play classical guitar and you worry that you are already in your forties and feel that you will be ancient by the time you have reached a decent proficiency then look at it this way: you will be as old as you were going to be anyway whether you start or not. So you might as well start taking lessons so that you can enjoy playing the *Concerto de Aranjuez* by Rodrigo in your old age.

It might be that now is not the right time for some of the things you need to gain, but it is still worth thinking about what they are so that they can sit in the outer reaches of your radar. Perhaps you need to wait until your children are of school age before you can consider going back to university to get the psychology degree that you need in order to work as a therapist. That's fine. In the meantime you can keep your dream alive by researching the available courses so that when the right time does arrive you can get straight on with applying for the best one for you.

Sometimes you discover some of the things you need to gain once your journey gets started. When I first started writing my novel I thought that all I needed was a fertile imagination and a reasonable command of the English language. It was only a few years later that I discovered that novel writing, and the sprinkling of clues that allow the reader to build up the ingredients of the story in their mind, was totally different to business writing where you just give the reader the information all in one chunk. I'm pretty good at the latter and still need to gain better skills at the former!

No matter how big your goals or one of the objects that you need to gain, there is always something you can do now towards it. Gemma's dream is to open up a café which specialises in serving locally grown, organic produce but first she needs to pay off some of her student debt. Initially she was down-hearted because it seemed like the debt repayment would take forever and she would never have her café. However we were able to identify some action that she could get started on immediately and she is now part way through a book-keeping course. Once that course is finished she wants to find a catering course that she can do at the weekend. In her spare time she researches potential suppliers and keeps an eye on property in the area of town where she would like to base her venture. These activities keep Gemma's dream alive and help her to feel that it will be possible to run a café at some point in the future. When that time does arrive she will be better prepared to meet the challenges that it will bring.

Make everyday reality part of your plan

When you gradually develop 'plan B' on the side, it helps you stay motivated in seeing through your current responsibilities. When one of my clients, Joseph, first started working with me he was finding it very difficult to get up in the morning and get to work on time. This meant that he had to stay later into the evening to catch up on his work and he was then caught in a circle of tiredness and tardiness. However, when he decided to take the plunge and start writing a book about his childhood he became motivated to get up earlier in the morning and write for an hour before work. Actually he found that once he had his writing pattern established it was so much easier for him to get out of bed that he was getting to work earlier than he used to before he started writing. He was then motivated to work hard during the day so that he could get everything done and get home earlier which in turn made it easier for him to get enough rest so that he could get up early the next morning. His writing shifted his whole motivation and he did not find his job as claustrophobic.

If it is not possible to work directly on your dream at the moment then see the overcoming of the obstacles that stand between you and your dream as part of the plan. For example, if you need to clear ten thousand pounds of credit card debt before you would be able to consider cutting down to a four day week in your day job then make that debt-reduction part of the journey towards your dream rather than seeing it as an obstacle to ever getting started. Knowing that paying off that debt is taking you closer to your goals may motivate you to find innovative ways to save money and help you endure some of the more frugal aspects that you need to impose on your lifestyle. The alternative is getting depressed because you think you are too broke to move forward with your life and this in turn may cost you more money as you try to medicate your pain with consumption or let your debt get further out of hand because you don't see a rosy future for yourself.

Your current job may have more value than you give it credit for in helping you achieve your dreams. For example it may be worth sticking with your current career for another two or three years and getting to the next level of management. The training that you will get and the experience of motivating a team as well as bringing in a project on time and on budget may prove to be valuable experience for when you run your own business. The achievements you build up in your day job may give you vital credibility for when you strike out on your own. I am entitled to put the letters ACA after my name which means I am a qualified chartered accountant. I never really wanted to train as an accountant, it was something that I ended up doing. Once I qualified I left the accountancy firm straight away and I have never worked as an accountant since then. Every year I pay £250 to remain a member of the Institute of Chartered Accountants and retain the right to keep the letters after my name. The direct debit for this subscription goes out on 2nd January which is the worst time for a lump of money to leave my bank account. Many a time I considered cancelling this subscription and my membership of the institute as all I ever seemed to do with those letters was sign passport photos for my friends and colleagues. However, when I started my coaching business my accountancy qualification and those letters gave me a lot of credibility. They indicated that I was not a life-coach of the tree-hugging variety and that I had a solid business background. This separated me from the competition and I have won business purely because I am a qualified accountant.

Exercise

In the space over the page write down what you need to gain in order to achieve your goals or dreams. You will probably think of ten things very easily. You may even be able to write fifteen without much effort. Once you have written down the gains that spring easily to mind, dig deep and see if you can come up with one or two more. Very often the ideas that you have to dredge up from the depths of your imagination turn out to be the most profound and hold the key to future success.

1. _____

2. _____

3. _____

4. _____

5. _____

6. _____

7. _____

8. _____

9. _____

10. _____

11. _____

12. _____

13. _____

14. _____

15. _____

Don't worry about how you will achieve these gains. The important thing is to identify them. In the chapters that follow you will start to get ideas on some easy tasks you can do now that will gradually bring those gains into your life.

Chapter 4:

What Do You Need To Lose?

What do you need to let go of?

So far we have talked about what you want for your life, or how to discover what you want, and in the last chapter we looked at what you needed to gain in order to have that dream or ideal life. Now we are going to examine the flip side of gains and determine what you may need to lose from your current life in order to achieve your dreams.

At the first *Lead The Life* workshop that I gave, I asked this same question: what do you need to lose or let go of in order to move towards your ideal life? One of my friends was participating in the workshop and he came straight out and said, "Ten hours a week of TV." If you want to win with your goals and build the life that you really want for yourself then there may be aspects of your current life that you have to drop and you may have to make some sacrifices in the short term.

Other answers to this question have been a stone in weight, working long hours, one day a week in the day job, the habit of saying yes to everything, the tendency of starting project after project but finishing none, fear of failure and fear of success. If the latter two answers resonate with you then you will be pleased to know that chapters six and seven will deal with fear, procrastination and unhelpful mindsets.

Exercise

In the space below make a list of what you need to lose from your life in order to achieve your goals and dreams. This list will be shorter than your list of gains and may include one or two profound insights.

1. _____

2. _____

3. _____

4. _____

5. _____

6. _____

7. _____

8. _____

9. _____

10. _____

If one of the losses that you wrote down feels a bit too drastic then figure out what you would need to gain to counteract this. Before having children Sally used to make bespoke suits for a living. She felt that it would be impossible to work at home again as a tailor without putting her adorable children on the losses list. Obviously this was not an option so the answer was that she needed to gain two days a week of childcare.

Sometimes it is necessary to negotiate some 'own time' within your family routine. Can you ring-fence three hours on a weekend to do your own thing or grab much needed sanity time? Perhaps you can train your family to understand that if the door to a specified room is closed then you can't be disturbed. Let them know up front what time you expect to emerge from your self-imposed cocoon and that you cannot be disturbed before that, not even if there is a phone call for you. Teaming up with a friend and having a rota of play dates may also buy you much needed time alone.

Another way of escaping the family for a few hours is to work in a garden shed. Many writers have used the shed as their studio including Roald Dahl, Phillip Pullman and Vic Reeves. The garden shed tends to be viewed as a male preserve but in the past three months I have visited two garden sheds used by women for professional purposes; the first being used for massage therapy, kinesiology and writing and the second one, which is more of a summer house than a shed, belongs to Mindy, my book coach, and we had a lovely morning planning the themes for this book in it. These were wonderful spaces and I am so inspired by them that I might consider one myself when I sell my London flat and buy a house with my boyfriend.

Another example of transposing a 'lose' to a 'gain' is in regards to health. For the last few years I have sometimes been plagued with a bad back. I don't like focussing on my bad back because the word 'bad' seems to stand out too much. Instead I like to put a more positive spin on the situation and work to gain a healthy and happy back instead. Some health conditions may never go away. As much as you would like to lose your lupus or your tinnitus or your dodgy knee, it may be easier to think about what you would need to gain in order to manage these conditions so that you are not held back by them. Depending on the condition it may be that you just need to gain some better habits – my back is much happier when I do a few minutes of stretching and core strength exercises and then it doesn't let me down. I have noticed that whenever I have a bad back episode it is always when I have become slack at doing these exercises. Thankfully since the last incident I have finally got into the habit of doing a few minutes a day so now I feel that I am gaining a happy and less-stressed back.

How many hats are you wearing?

We all have an identity and this identity forms the labels we use to describe ourselves. Examples of identities are wife, mother, accountant, teacher, chairman of the committee, bread-winner, fat, thin, healthy, old, young, menopausal, fit, tall, short, tone-deaf, artistic, pregnant, parent, infertile, single, divorced, manager, banker, professional, blue-collar, white-collar, working class, black, white, Chinese, atheist, Jewish, religious, busy or lazy. One person will have several identities and these will include those that the person perceives of themselves as well as those placed on them by others. The way we view our identities may shape our life experience and our beliefs about what kind of life and future we are entitled to have.

How many hats are you currently wearing? Which of these do you genuinely enjoy and which ones do you resent? Which ones are you desperately hiding behind and which ones are you desperately clinging onto? Which ones could you let go of to make space for your dream identity and which ones *must* you let go of in order to move forwards?

One of my clients, Tom, described himself as a busy person, one of life's 'do-ers'. His dream was to write a book about fitness but he never seemed to find the time to get started on it. Among the many hats that he wore was being secretary for his local rugby club. He used to enjoy this role but over time it had become a chore and he began to resent the way other committee members always assumed that 'good old Tom' would get on with any jobs that needed doing. Tom found himself being increasingly jealous of his friend, Bill who had written three novels, though none of them were published. The catalyst came when after many years of receiving rejection letters, Bill finally received an offer from a publisher. Tom really wanted the same opportunity for himself so he made the decision to resign as secretary from the rugby club. He also quit his role on his local residents association and started saying no to other requests that would have eaten a lot of his time. These changes freed up his schedule. He now spends between eight and ten hours a week writing his book and recently completed the first draft of his manuscript.

One way of ascertaining whether a role that you play can be dropped is to observe your use of the word 'should'. For example:

"I really should pop round and see Margaret."

"I should stay behind and get these meeting notes finished."

"I should stick with training to be a solicitor because I'll earn more money."

"I should support Mary and go on that protest march with her."

"I should knuckle down and get on with my studying."

From these examples it is clear that whoever is making the statement really does not want to do what they are telling themselves they should do. This person doesn't want to see Margaret, they're ambivalent about the protest march even though Mary is passionate about it and no wonder they are having trouble applying themselves to the studying or being conscientious at work – they don't want to be a solicitor!

If you catch yourself saying or thinking 'should' a lot, then examine the hat that the 'should' belongs to and decide whether you want to keep wearing it or whether you could starting ditching this hat in favour of a more exciting one. To combat a 'should' substitute the word 'could' instead. This gives you choice. "I could go and see Margaret." Now you can willingly go and visit Margaret or decide not to. "I could continue with my training to be a solicitor, or I could do something more interesting even though the financial prospects may not be as lucrative." Now you can make an informed choice about your career rather than stick with something you hate and spend many years resenting it.

Sometimes it isn't possible to completely shed an identity but it may be possible to lose it for a day or a few hours. Perhaps your relationship would benefit from having a child-free weekend away or you might need a break from caring for an aged relative and escape to do your own thing for a few hours. Sheila had always wanted to paint. At school she had enjoyed art and did it at A' level. Ten years ago having stopped working to become a mother and then waiting until the youngest began primary school, she had very excitedly started an eighteen month art foundation course. Unfortunately her marriage ended twelve months into the course and she had to abandon it and go back into the workforce as a legal secretary. Not much art had been made since but now that her eldest child was at university and the middle one was living with his father she wondered whether it was possible to start painting again. She found a Saturday morning portraiture class at her local further education college. Although her youngest was still at home, the fact that she spent every other weekend at her father's meant that Sheila only had to ensure that her daughter was suitably occupied every second Saturday. Sheila worshipped her children and was very proud at how she had raised them on her own, but she loved those art classes because once a week for three and a half hours she was 'Sheila the artist' not 'Mum where's me favourite trainers'.

Conversely, maybe you could borrow an identity or have it on a pretend basis for a few hours a week. Dave had long since given up on making it as a professional musician but he loved it when he came across a group of similar middle-aged wannabes who lived out the dream of playing in a rock band every Sunday afternoon in a basement pool room. Cindy never met Mr Right in time to have her own children but she enjoys the opportunity to be a big kid when she takes her niece and nephew to the park every Saturday. In fact she is going to ask her brother if he would be happy for her to cart them off to Disneyland in Paris in their next half-term break. Tanya loves fashion but doesn't earn enough to wear designer labels on a regular basis. However, recently she got a bonus at work and splashed out on a pair of the highest heeled Jimmy Choos she could find. Every time she wears them she feels like she is strutting down the runway even though she is really tottering down Tooting Broadway on the way to catch the tube.

You might be holding on to an old identity which stops you from enjoying a new one. I was at a conference recently and got chatting to a man who had lost eight stone in weight over the previous thirteen months. He felt and looked so much healthier and his doctor no longer pronounced his cholesterol levels to be a death sentence. However, he had one problem. Whenever he went shopping for clothes, and he needed a complete new wardrobe having lost so much weight, he never managed to buy anything which flattered his new figure. Buying suits and work shirts was okay because these were sized in formal measurements and he knew what they were. It was casual clothes that were giving him a problem. We chatted about beliefs and identity and then the penny dropped for him – he still saw himself as a heavily overweight person and therefore kept on assuming that he couldn't wear slim cut shirts and knitwear or straight cut jeans. Even though he had been successful in losing so much weight he hadn't yet adopted the mindset of a svelte shopper with a good figure who could enjoy wearing stylish, well-made clothes.

Alternatively the presence of an old identity may be sabotaging your best efforts to make positive changes in your life. This is very common with people who have given up smoking. Even though months or years go by since they last had a cigarette they still think of themselves as a smoker and in a moment of weakness they revert back to this identity.

Occasionally you may need to let go of a friendship or relationship. Some friendships do run their course. Your time together might have been perfect for a particular era in your life, but perhaps it is not right for the future. It can be very painful to sever the links with a person and it can also be very liberating.

Maybe you don't need to cut someone off completely, and in the case of a family member this may not be possible, but you do need to set new boundaries on how you interact with them.

Exercise

Review your list of losses from the last exercise and consider whether you need to put any hats or identities on this list. Also think about whether you need to add any new identities to your list of gains in the previous chapter.

Are your values in line with your life?

Your values are the principles in life that are important to you. They are who you are. They represent your unique and individual essence. When you are able to live in accordance with your values you feel fulfilled and in tune with your higher self or with the rhythm of the universe. Your life contains a wonderfully creative undercurrent. If however you are not living in accordance with your values then you are likely to feel stressed, ill, out of rhythm, blocked, depressed or trapped.

Your values are what make you tick and the make-up of life that feels right to you. They may incorporate a moral code but are not wholly defined by this; your values are a more universal expression of your essential self.

Values are intangible. They are not an action or a possession. Money is not a value, although the qualities it brings to your life such as security, freedom or fun are values. Designer clothes are not a value but they may represent your values of achievement, joy or creativity. Similarly, a modest wardrobe of more regular, high-street apparel may be evidence of your values of thrift, contentment or practicality. Your family and friends are not values but love and friendship are. Travel is not a value but it might be evidence of your values of adventure, spirituality or learning.

In order to know if you are living in a way which is congruent with your values, you need to know what they are. When you know what they are, and which are the most important to you, then you can make decisions about how you can bring your life closer to them. In the exercise below you are going to identify your values and then rank them in order of importance.

Exercise – Part One

From the list below and over the page circle twelve values that are important to you. There are no wrong answers in this exercise – your values are personal to you and no one is going to judge you for your choices. Use your gut reaction to decide whether or not the value is important to you. You will know what the wording of each value means to you.

Acceptance	Influence
Achievement	Integrity
Adventure	Justice
Beauty	Kindness
Brotherhood	Knowledge
Charity	Leadership
Comfort	Learning
Community	Legacy

Contentment	Love
Creativity	Making a difference
Development	Parenting
Dignity	Patriotism
Discipline	Peace
Discovery	Power
Esteem	Practicality
Family	Relaxation
Freedom	Security
Friendship	Self confidence
Fun	Self expression
Generosity	Service
Giving	Sisterhood
God	Spirituality
Growth	Strength
Happiness	Success
Health	Thrift
Honesty	Time alone
Honour	Travel
Humility	Truth
Independence	Using my talents
Individuality	Wisdom

Exercise – Part Two

Now that you have your values, we need to find their order of importance. Of the values that you circled in part one, select six of them and write them in order of importance in the space below. Again, there are no wrong answers here. These are your values and you can have them in the order which is most significant to you. Be honest with yourself and don't put a value near the top of the list because you think it should be at the top. Go with what you really think and feel. If you can't decide between one value or another just go with your gut instinct.

1. _____

2. _____

3. _____

4. _____

5. _____

6. _____

You now have your values and you know which is the most important. You may be surprised at what is most important and what is less important. That's the whole point of doing the exercise: to see what is *really* important to you and what matters less. Even though you picked six from the original twelve that you circled that doesn't mean that the others aren't important too.

Does your life reflect your values? If security was one of

your top values and you are in a sales or commission based role, then you are probably feeling a bit stressed. Similarly, if flexibility, self-expression or creativity is one of your uppermost values and you work, for example, in the public sector in a highly controlled environment then you may feel like a caged bird.

If the balance of your life does reflect your values then congratulations. If not, then what adjustments would you need to make to bring your life closer to them? Your values order can help you make decisions concerning how you prioritise your time. I have come across several clients whose values related to their job were towards the bottom of their priority and yet they worked long hours or made many personal sacrifices for their job. It is only when they saw their values in black and white that they could see where they were going wrong and could then make decisions about how to re-prioritise their life.

Sometimes a busy period at work is unavoidable and some professions require more than a nine to five commitment. However, it is still possible to juggle work so that you have time for other priorities. Even though it may not be realistic to leave the office on the dot of five every night, perhaps you could do it once or twice during the week. That way you have some evening time for family, friends, hobbies or building your dream on the side and you are still satisfying the demands of your job. Again, I have found for myself and witnessed with my clients, when you can carve out some time to do the activities you enjoy then work is not as stressful and it is easier to see the benefits that your job provides for you.

Knowing your values also helps you to make decisions about what would be a good career for you. When I have clients who have no idea what they want for their future, I find that eliciting their values gives them some concrete knowledge about themselves. This can then be used as a yardstick to see how different career ideas measure up to the type of person they are and how their needs can be satisfied.

Your values are not set in stone and can move around depending on your age and whether your circumstances change. For example, having freedom as a value near the top of the list is fine, until you lose the job that gave you the money to have the financial ability to do all the things you love. In this situation you might find that security suddenly becomes higher priority as a value, at least until you can find another job. Security may also move up the list if you have a baby on the way, or it might move down your list if you finish paying off your mortgage. It is therefore useful to repeat the values exercise from time to time as it may give you some signposts on how to prioritise what you currently need from a job, profession or lifestyle.

Exercise
In the light of your values, review once again your gains and losses to see if you need to add any items to these lists.

You may find that you've had some profound insights into your life as a result of reading this chapter and doing the exercises. And you may have uncovered some facets of yourself or some tendencies that you don't like. It is good to know these truths even though they may feel unpalatable, but don't beat yourself up over them or expect big changes of yourself over night. A gradual transition in your thinking and behaviour, probably with some setbacks, is okay. It can take time to turn around a large ship and alter its course. It is liberating to realise what you are no longer willing to tolerate and accept for yourself.

chapter 5:

Time To Build An Action Plan

I once read an article in a magazine about Alexandra Tolstoy (1884 – 1979) who was the youngest daughter of the Russian writer, Leo Tolstoy (1828 – 1910). Like her father she was very concerned with the rights and welfare of ordinary people and had been frequently imprisoned by the authorities before she fled Russia in 1929. Whilst still living in Russia she had bought some land and decided to build a school and a 200 bed hospital on it. However, such were the conditions that she needed to make the bricks herself. In order to make bricks she needed to make a kiln and in order to heat the kiln she needed firewood. Therefore, one of her first tasks in this noble mission was to chop wood.

It doesn't matter how large or lofty your goals are, or how scary or daunting they may be, they will still require action on a set of tasks that may be as humble as chopping wood. The beauty of such a task is that it is easy to do and as you complete the task you can feel satisfied that you are on your way to achieving great endeavours.

If Alexandra was about to chop the wood today she might discover that she did not have the right tools to hand in which case her initial task would have been to jump in the car and head out to the nearest hardware store, or perhaps she would have gone on the internet, done a Google search on where to purchase an axe, and ordered what she needed online.

With many of my clients, I have noticed that the very first step they need to perform is also an internet search for whatever course or information that will lead them towards their goals. A search is very easy to do, it isn't scary and it doesn't actually commit you to handing in your notice or investing in a qualification – but it does whet your appetite for new beginnings and it also helps you break through the procrastination barrier and actually get started on something.

You've probably gathered that this chapter is about taking action. However, I would like to congratulate you on the action that you have already taken. For starters, you went out and bought or borrowed this book. You have stuck with it for four chapters and hopefully you will have done the exercises too. Congratulations on your progress thus far and let us see what other actions you can now take towards your dreams. In the last couple of chapters you have ascertained what you need to gain and what you need to let go of in order to lead your dream life. Now you need to figure out what you can start doing at the moment in order to achieve these gains and losses.

What is one, really easy action that you can do right now that will put you on the journey towards your dreams?

Now put this book down and go and do it right now … go on off you go … now … go do it!

Have you done it? No cheating! How does it feel?

I'm guessing that some of you haven't yet put the book down and done something constructive towards your dream. Never mind, I'm sure that you will soon be inspired to do so! In the meantime you can do the exercise below and construct an action plan.

Exercise

In the space opposite write down every action that you can think of that will help you to achieve your gains and losses. If you have a gain or loss and you have no idea how to achieve it, don't worry about that at this stage. Just write down the actions that you do know about.

Examples of actions you may take are:

- Ring up local college to see if any places are available on a creative writing course.
- Book an appointment with hypnotherapist for a 'stop smoking' session.
- Go and see HR at work to enquire about possibility of doing a four day week.
- Find out about computer courses.
- Put aside extra £15 a week towards paying off debt.
- Get a subscription to an investment magazine.
- Phone Eileen and ask her about knitting machines.
- Book another driving test and set up another group of lessons.
- Join a marketing mastermind group.
- Make one sales call every day.
- Ring up a local osteopath and ask which training option they think is the best one.
- Buy a book on meditation.
- Google wind-surfing lessons.

Actions for next 7 days:

Actions for next 8 – 14 days:

Actions for next 15 - 30 days:

Actions for next 31 - 60 days:

Actions for next 61 - 90 days:

Actions for next 91 - 180 days:

Actions for next 181 - 365 days:

Actions for next 1 – 2 years:

You will probably find that you have more actions written down for the first two time periods: next seven days and eight to fourteen days. Return to those sections and decide exactly when you will perform those tasks. You may need to consult your diary or a calendar. You can jot the timing down next to each task if you wish.

What else would assist you in making sure those first few tasks get done? Do you need to communicate to anyone else the time commitment you require to do these tasks? Is it worth enlisting the help from a friend who can ask you how it is going or nag you if you start procrastinating? Do you need to set any reminders on your phone or computer to indicate that it is time to work on your goals or dreams?

Do not worry if the timing slips on some of your longer range tasks. You may have heard that most people overestimate what they can accomplish in a year but underestimate what they can achieve in a decade. That gives you plenty of time to catch up.

Beat procrastination now

It is easy to find reasons to procrastinate – that's why this chapter has focussed on some easy initial steps to get you moving on taking action towards your dreams and goals. Sometimes we procrastinate because we worry about problems we might have further down the line with a goal and use this as an excuse not to bother starting. For example, Lucien was worrying about how he will ever satisfy the demand for the emerald and pewter earrings that he planned to make as part of his jewellery business. What if they are the bestselling line and he can't make them quick enough?

He could take on someone else to do that but then he will have to train them and pay them and they may not make them in the same way as he does which means people may not want to buy them after all and then he will be stuck with all the overheads and a sack full of unwanted earrings so therefore perhaps it's best not to start the venture in the first place!

When I was first starting out towards my dreams one of the best pieces of advice I heard was don't bother worrying about a problem that you haven't yet got. For Lucien, the problem of satisfying demand for a specific earring does not yet exist so it would be better for him to work on more immediate concerns, like finishing his jewellery making course or finding ways to spend less time at the his day job thus leaving more him time to produce jewellery. Then one day in the future if that problem does occur he can celebrate the fact that his designs are so successful and no doubt, at that time, he will have it within his capacity to find a solution to making the pieces fast enough. Maybe his customers will be happy to join a waiting list and pay a higher price for the privilege of wearing his jewellery or maybe he will outsource production to China and revel in the fact that he is now supplying half a dozen high street stores with his designs.

Beware that this expression of a future problem may come from someone else: your partner, parent or someone else who is close to you. Do not be knocked off course by their doubts. Just smile at them, tell them that you only worry about problems that you actually have right now and reassure them that you will be able to figure out a way through should that situation arise in the future.

Procrastination can also rear its head because you feel that you don't know all of the steps that you need to take. You find yourself in a panic that you aren't clear on what step number eighty-one is so you had better not start on anything because you don't want to get to the eightieth step and then get stalled! Again, this is worrying about a problem that you don't yet have. Just get started on what you do know because each stage of the way forward will reveal itself to you when you need it. One way or another you will learn more or bump into just the right person who has the right information for you at the right time or you will figure out where you can go for help.

Working towards your dreams is like crossing a bridge. The bridge is going to take you from where you are now to where you would rather be. Even if you can't see the details of every single paving stone of the bridge so long as you can see the first one or two that is all you need. Once you have stepped on them then you will be able to see paving stones three and four and so on. Providing you keep putting one foot in front of the other then you will get to the other side. Some parts of the bridge may be a little scary or even treacherous, and other parts will be exhilarating and have a great view. From time to time you will look back and be amazed at how far you have travelled and eventually you will touch down on the other side. You will probably find some interesting companions on the bridge and you can ease your journey by travelling together or by using them as your guide.

Sometimes you may feel overwhelmed at every thing you need to do and how you are going to fit taking action around your existing responsibilities. The best way to cope with this is to pick any one of the tasks, or a small section of it, and just get it done. You will feel better for having completed something and again, one task at a time, you will begin to see that you are making progress. It doesn't matter how long it takes you to achieve your dreams, it just matters that you start taking some action and continue as often as you can.

Mother Teresa was once asked by an interviewer how she coped with all the people that needed her attention. She responded that she just helped one person at a time. This reminds me of the Jewish expression of one who saves a single life saves the whole world. In taking action towards your dreams you don't have to do everything all at once nor do you have to be all things to all people. When you overcome your resistance and tackle one task at a time you are already making the causes to complete the others.

If you are the type of person who starts many projects and finishes none of them then give some thought to what action you could take toward bringing just one of them to completion. It doesn't matter what project you choose as the satisfaction of finishing one undertaking will give you momentum to complete another. In order to get a project completed, you can apply the same methodology as we have used to scope out your goals: quickly write down what you want the completed project to be, then think about what you would need to gain in order for that to happen and what you would need to lose or let go of. Finally, come up with one or two easy actions that you can start right now and you are on your way to completion. Even if you had to run through this process on a daily basis until the project is done, wouldn't it be worth it to have the fulfilment at actually having completed something?

Keeping track of your action and progress

As human beings we respond well to success and the feeling of achievement. One way that you can have this is to give yourself the satisfaction of ticking off the items on your action plan one by one as you complete them. There are other ways of tracking your progress and you can experiment to see if any of those listed below suit you:

1. Use a diary

A diary, whether on paper or on a computer, is a very useful way of planning when you intend to perform an activity towards your goals. You can use it to plan when you will have spare time to do some of the tasks from your action plan, and if necessary schedule into your diary for them. This helps with your commitment to yourself and it may also indicate to others when you are busy and are not free for other pursuits. You may also want to plan out some milestone dates and then figure out the activities that need to be completed in order to reach your milestones.

2. Mark off activity on a calendar

Someone told me about this tip a few years ago when I was struggling to write on a consistent basis. You take a calendar (this works better with a paper calendar rather than an online version though you could always print one off from your computer) and in the case of writing mark a big red W on each day that you write. This idea appealed to me because I was marking up when I had actually done some writing rather than when I intended to do it. I soon found that I got competitive with myself and tried to get as many Ws in each week as I could. I have also used similar techniques to indicate when I have done marketing activities in my business and I currently like to tick off daily that I have done exercises that keep my back happy and healthy. You can decide for yourself the nature of the activity that you would like to track and which symbol would be most appropriate to mark up on your calendar.

The act of physically ticking a chart is a very simple yet

effective way of taking committed action. At the end of each week you can then have a review session with yourself and see whether you had sufficient ticks for the week or whether you can improve on your score in the following week.

3. Use a journal

Journalling is a great way to motivate yourself, discuss your hopes and fears and reflect on the progress you are making. Writing a page or two first thing in the morning is a very effective way of sifting your thoughts and deciding on your priorities for the day. Another way of using a journal is to spend a few minutes before you go to bed reflecting on what action you have taken during the day. Even if you have just done one small thing such as look for a piece of information on the internet or sent a relevant email then it is good to positively re-enforce to yourself that you are making progress. If you reported back to yourself every day for three months you would be surprised at how much you will have accomplished.

It is also very powerful at the end of the day to write down three things for which you are grateful that day. Having gratitude is a wonderful way to keep your mind positive and to notice small blessings and stepping stones, even if you are facing challenges or obstacles.

4. Use online scheduling tools

You can also use your computer or mobile phone to maintain a task list. Programmes such as Outlook allow you to enter tasks and set due dates. If you sync between your computer and a smart phone such as the Blackberry or iPhone then these tasks also come across so that you can conveniently update and maintain them on your phone. When I have a major project running, whether of a business or personal nature, I often keep a task list in programmes such as Excel. Then when I have some time to spend on the project I can choose one of the tasks that I fancy doing at that time. I find that this helps me to keep my focus on the project and it makes efficient use of the time that I have available. Again, it is satisfying to see the list reduce in size as I delete the items one by one as I complete them.

In addition to standard Microsoft or Apple computer tools there are also activity packages and time management software that you can download to scope out and manage your tasks.

If you track your progress you are likely to proceed at a quicker pace towards your goals and it will feel as though they are more achievable. In my quest to lose weight one of the key components in my success has been tracking not only the food that I consume but my physical activity and my weight loss progress to date. I do this all in one notebook which has a section for each of these components. Many studies have shown that keeping a food diary is an effective weight loss tool. Writing down everything I eat helps me to stick to the food plan and make a decision about when to have a splurge and treat myself. I really enjoy the weekly ritual of having an official weigh-in and entering the results in my book. Even when my weight has gone up by a pound or two or stayed the same, I still find it useful to write it down in my book and continue with the plan. Much like putting the Ws on the writing calendar I described earlier, I find a bit of self-competition useful when tracking my physical activity and seeing how one week's activity compares to another and to study the correlation to the weight loss for that week. In short, writing down everything about the weight loss has helped me to see my weekly progress, pick myself up when I have faltered and stay accountable to myself and my goals.

Finally, your written progress notes provide an historic record of your achievements. It can be very encouraging when you look back over these notes and they may well spur you on if you hit a difficult patch down the line. They serve as a constant reminder that you are moving forward and that your efforts are paying off.

Accountability

You can also stoke up your accountability by committing to someone else that you will get certain tasks done. You are more likely to complete a task when you have you have told someone else that will do it. You may well find yourself frantically taking action at the last minute so that you can report back positively but don't worry about this, at least the action is done and you are moving forward. Without the power of accountability you may not have bothered!

When you are working towards your dreams it can be very effective to buddy up with someone else who is striving towards a goal and make commitments to each other. They don't have to be aiming towards the same goals as you but it is good if they, like you, really want to achieve their dreams. You can meet in person or arrange meetings by phone at a time interval that suits the two of you, be that weekly, monthly or quarterly. At each meeting you will each report back on your progress and then specify new tasks that you will go on to complete prior to the next meeting.

Alternatively you can enter into a formal arrangement with a coach. Some coaches work in what is called a non-directive way which means that you set your agenda and pace and they hold you to your commitments. Other coaches are more directive, particularly if they have specialist knowledge from which you wish to benefit, and they may tell you what you need to do and by when. Either way, you are likely to progress at a faster pace than if left to your own devices and there is less chance that you will give up on working towards your goals.

Whether you are accountable to a coach or to a buddy, one of the benefits of this arrangement is that you have someone to whom you can give quick updates on your progress. Again, this can help with getting things done. Many a time if a client is struggling to complete a task or is a bit scared or daunted by it I say to them, "Would it help if you emailed me when you've done it?" and then I pin them down to when I might expect that email. Notice that they are reporting to me, not me emailing them a reminder. When you have committed to someone else that you will do something you have a natural urge to want to please that person, so you are more likely to do the task to fulfil your promise of letting them know it is done. It also feels good when you get the "well done" response back from your coach or buddy. I know this because as well as being a coach I also have one. At the moment I take great pleasure in emailing Mindy telling her when I have completed a chapter and letting her know the current word count of my manuscript. Knowing that I have to have a formal conversation with her every ten to fourteen days about the book also gives me the incentive to make time to sit at my computer and keep typing!

Congratulations once again on making it this far through the book and pat yourself on the back for all the action you have taken. Some people never dare to believe that their dreams are possible much less start to do something about them. You are now way ahead of the game. Well done!

In part two we will look at how to overcome obstacles such as fear, lack of confidence, time and money. From these you will learn more about yourself as well as pick up more hints and tips to help you stick with your action plan and continue your journey.

part TWO

Chapter 6:

Keep Your Head Happy

The battle between head and heart

Imagine two people sitting together and having a chat: Nathan and Ray.

Nathan: I've got this brilliant idea for an amazing gadget which helps women's hair to grow faster.

Ray: That sounds interesting. How does it work?

Nathan: Oh it's so clever. It's this special piece of cloth which you lay on your pillow at night, then as you sleep on it your hair grows by a whole centimetre. I'm gonna get so rich when I sell it.

Ray: Gosh, are you sure it's safe? You wouldn't want to get sued if it had any adverse affects.

Nathan: Oh it'll be fine. We'll do all the proper tests on it. Actually I'm really excited about testing it because I have a feeling that it will cure baldness too. Imagine that!

Ray: Clinical trials can be expensive you know. You'll have to convince the medical profession to endorse it. How will you get the money to develop it?

Nathan: I'll go on that TV show, Dragons' Den, and pitch it there. They'll love it. The market for it is huge. It's going to change the lives of so many people. Women will be able to completely change their hairstyles in just a few days and they won't have to shell out on hair extensions if they want long hair.

Ray: Those guys on Dragons Den are tough cookies. You're going to have to know what your exact production costs are and how big your market really is and even if it is a big earner you'll have to sell a huge chunk of your business to one of them if you want their backing. It's a lot of hassle and you might not get as much back as you want.

Nathan: So what if they take their share. This is huge. That'll still leave plenty for me – especially if the baldness cure bit pans out. Wow, can you imagine the market for that?

Ray: Yes – but you said a crucial word – if. At the moment you've no idea if it will work or not. And what if they think you're crazy and don't want to go for the idea. Then you'll be humiliated. They might laugh in your face. Are you sure you can handle that?

And so the conversation continued. Nathan, ever the optimist, so excited at how he can solve hair woes for the masses and Ray, concerned that Nathan hasn't thought this through properly, is taking on more than he can handle and worried that Nathan could end up humiliated.

This is the type of dialogue that goes on inside us, between our head and our heart, every time we have a yearning from deep within to improve ourselves or answer a higher calling that may make a valuable contribution to humanity. Our heart is positive, excited and altruistic yet our head reels from the effect that the idea may have on our lives and goes, "That's all very well but…" and tells us all the reasons why we shouldn't do it.

Mostly our head wins. We look at the practicalities, the mortgage, time and money, and our head tells our heart that it's just not possible at the moment. Life continues and the idea is buried – until the next time it surfaces and then we go through the whole process again and the head still wins. Perhaps the head wins a couple more times. On each occasion that the heart is defeated it is like a noose tightening around it one notch at a time. Its flow of blood, oxygen and life-force is constricted. Eventually the heart is so sad that it can take no more. It either shrivels to nothing causing illness and depression to take hold, or it decides to have one last almighty attempt at being heard and makes such a huge noise, causing major ructions in the status quo and it won't stop causing chaos until it is finally listened to. Maybe by then it is still possible to act on its desires or maybe it is too late.

Negotiating with your head

Why do we inflict this cruelty on our heart? On my very first date with my boyfriend we were ambling along the South Bank in London and decided to wander into one of the bookshops. As we came to the popular psychology, self help section he said: "I need to sort my head out before I dare listen to my heart." Why are we so fearful of what our head thinks?

What if there was a way that we could listen to our heart and keep our head happy? I believe that we need to enter into negotiations with our head. In the battle between head and heart, the head is often cast as the bad guy and yet for all its negativity, it is only trying to protect us and look after our best interests. It is not intentionally out to strangle our heart, it is just afraid.

For many years Peter had been troubled by all the homeless people that he saw when he came into London every day to his accountancy job. He often saw the same young man sitting on a dirty blanket in the subways of Blackfriars tube station. Sometimes he gave him money as he passed him, other times he stared straight ahead and kept walking. He constantly wrestled with himself as to what would be the best way to help the young man and others like him. He sometimes thought about approaching his employer to see if there was a way they could give employment to one or two homeless people thus helping them to break the no job, no home cycle. Other times he even thought about setting up a charity that would act as broker between employers and the homeless, again to help place them in some kind of work. But he never got around to acting on either of these ideas. When he came to one of my workshops he said he was bored at work having reached a senior management position at his firm and he wanted to find a way of doing something more meaningful with his life. As a result of the exercises in the workshop his ideas to help the homeless surfaced once again. When I asked him what stopped him acting on this he came out with a list of worries: he didn't want to raise the issue at work in case it got turned down; yet if they agreed to give a job to the young man in the subway and it didn't work out then it would reflect badly on him; if he set up a charity then how would he find the time to get it off the ground and what if he enjoyed his charity work so much that he

76

no longer wanted to stay in his well paid accountancy job. These were all rational fears where his head was finding good reasons to protect him from any downside of following the desires of his heart.

We had a conversation about his head and his heart and I asked him what reassurance his head would need in order to be sure that nothing bad would happen if he acted on one of these ideas. Peter replied that his head needed to know that his job and hence his income was not at stake. I asked him what the risk was of him losing his job if he enquired about whether it would be possible to give a chance of employment to a homeless person. He smiled and said that there was zero risk of this happening.

Then I asked him what was the worst that could happen if his firm were able to offer the young man in the subway a job and it turned out that the young man really wasn't that employable. Peter replied that he might lose a little bit of face, but since he wouldn't have been the only person taking the decision on such a scheme and that anyone involved in the decision would know that they were taking a risk on employing such a person, probably not much would happen other than facing the sadness of not being able to help the young man. Then he added that perhaps the firm would then help the young man in other ways such as finding him a place to live or sponsoring some kind of treatment for him if that was required. We had established that there was no chance of Peter losing his job. When I asked him if his head felt happier about this, he nodded.

Then we talked about his idea of setting up a charity. I asked him if he set up the charity, would he have to give up his job and his income. No, he replied. Is your head is happy with that, I asked. Yes, he replied, though he said he would need to find time to do it. I asked him what his head thought would be needed to make the time burden easier. He replied straightaway that his head suggested that he find a like-minded person from within his firm or approach friends at other accountancy firms to set something up and divide the work between them. Then his mind raced on to how he could use the Institute of Chartered Accountants to draw attention to the scheme and get potential employers involved. And then he thought of how his university alumni association could also be used to publicise the charity. We laughed that his head seemed to have some pretty good ideas on how to go about achieving this desire.

I posed another question to Peter: if his charity took off and got substantial backing from some blue chip firms, who would be the best person in terms of experience and passion to head it up and take care of its finances? He replied that he would love to be financial director of such a charity. Can financial directors of a charity make a decent salary, I asked. Well yes, he replied, it's a specialist job and you need to pay the right money to get the right person. I asked him if his head would be happy with that. Yes, said Peter, and my heart would be very happy too.

If you have a chat with your head, examine its fears and see what solutions you could put in place to mitigate those fears, you would be surprised at what it will agree to! Even if it won't let you launch full steam ahead into pursuing your dreams it might be happy for you to dip your toe into the waters of your heart's desire and try out a version of your aspirations with which it feels safe.

Exercise
Find somewhere comfortable to sit in a quiet, private place where you won't be disturbed. Hold your hands out in front of you.

In one hand imagine that you are holding your heart and in the other, imagine that you are holding your head. In your imagination they don't have to literally look like a heart or a brain, just something that represents these two roles. You can give them names if you wish.

Now facilitate a conversation between them. Ask your heart what it would love to do and then listen to your head's reaction. Allow your head the space to voice its fears, however irrational or silly they may be, and reassure it that you are not judging the fears. Let your head and heart negotiate together to find a way that keeps your head happy and allows your heart some freedom to start following its desires.

You may find that as your head and heart reach a consensus your hands naturally move closer to each other. You may even want to join your hands together. As they reach agreement thank them both very much for participating in the conversation and sharing their ideas with each other and with yourself. Let them know that they can have a similar conversation at any point in the future if it is necessary.

Your inner gremlin moves in mysterious ways

The fears that your head goes through when your heart is pushing for you to act from your soul may be rational or irrational. It is as though you are carrying around your own special gremlin whose only purpose is to thwart your deeply cherished desires and yearnings. The inner gremlin is our small ego and it wants our life to be safe, contained, and without risk or surprises. If it senses that we are about to listen to our hearts then it needs to act swiftly and put a stop to what it considers to be madness, immediately.

As we have already seen, one of the ways that the gremlin

gets in our way is to put lots of questions, 'buts' and reasons not to proceed into our head. It also acts in more subtle ways. It may show up as illness, a sudden busy period at work just when you were going to have a bit more time to yourself or an accident. Illness has often reared its ugly head for me when I am on the verge of making a creative breakthrough. This first surfaced when I was a music student preparing for my final degree recital. My first instrument was the flute and I was the underdog amongst the other three flautists in my year. I was desperate to prove how fabulous a flute player I was in my recital and yet for the last few weeks leading up to it, and throughout my final exams, I was bogged down with a viral-type exhaustion illness and was extremely pained by the fact that in the end I only gave a mediocre performance. Years later when I started to write, and again wanted to show my creative brilliance to the world, the gremlin surfaced as repetitive strain injury. This was quite scary as my passion was writing and I earned my money by computer programming, both activities relied on me being able to use a computer keyboard. By this point I had been practising Buddhism for many years, and I had developed an understanding of such issues. I understood the nature of the inner gremlin and that obstacles will occur when you are answering your heart's calling. I knew that I was suffering from an inner-generated resistance and that I just needed to keep moving forward as best as I could in spite of the RSI. With this determination, over the period of a few months I found the right medical treatment and postural supports to use at my computer, and the condition became manageable.

Sometimes the gremlin might get at us via other people. It might be that when you are about to devote time to what you really want to do, someone close to you will have some kind of illness or emergency which ends up encroaching on the time you had put aside for yourself. This can happen to our nearest and dearest when they see the status quo changing and their gremlin starts to act up.

The gremlin can also show up as self-doubt. You may feel that you never know enough to launch yourself as a consultant, or that you need to take yet another course before you feel confident in your abilities.

Another way of viewing the gremlin is that it represents our fear. I like to classify fear in two ways: tangible and intangible. When I looked up fear in the thesaurus it gives synonyms such as *terror, dread, horror, worry, panic* and *phobia*. I classify these types of fear as tangible fear. If a spider or a mouse were to run across the floor right now you may be frightened of it. If you have to ask your bad-tempered boss for a pay-rise then you may feel a sense of trepidation. If you have just dented your partner's prized car then you may feel scared about breaking the news to them. We are all familiar with these types of fear.

However, you may not be familiar with the fear caused by the inner gremlin, what I like to call intangible fear. This is why it can be dangerous. I call intangible fear the carbon monoxide of fear because you can't touch, smell or taste it but over time it can strangle the life-force out of all your plans and desires. If you don't know about the workings of the inner gremlin and your own special version of self-sabotage, then you don't know when you are falling prey to it.

In my early thirties, during my Bridget Jones era, for a couple of years I had a pattern of dating men who were based overseas, mainly in America. I was forever jumping on planes to have snatched weekend dates in far off places and ran up huge phone bills in between those meetings. I did not see this as a problem as it reflected the way that I travelled in my work as an investment banker and I believed at that time that one did not choose who one fell in love with, it just happened. One of these men in particular captured my heart. I wanted to marry him, have his babies and move to his homeland state of Louisiana. Unfortunately he did not feel the same way about me though in my eyes we did seem to have some special connection and many of our colleagues thought we were having a secret affair. His reluctance to enter into a proper relationship with me caused me a huge amount of pain and I regularly lamented about this to my friends.

My best friend made the observation to me that one of the reasons I was single was because I kept choosing men who were not only geographically unavailable, but were also pretty flaky on the commitment stakes. She felt that this reflected my own fear of commitment. At that time I could not understand what she was saying as I was desperate to be with Mr Louisiana, so how could I possibly have a fear of commitment? Over the next few years my pattern continued of falling for men who seemed to like me, though not enough to actually go out with me. Finally, the penny suddenly dropped. I understood what my friend had meant and at last I could see my own fear of revealing myself warts and all to another person. That meant that I kept meeting men who were the mirror of myself in that they too were scared to take me on.

This repeating pattern was intangible fear. I kept doing it but I could not see the pattern. It prevented me from finding true and rewarding love as well as having children because I wasted my fertile years mooning about over men who were never going to commit to me.

We are the last people to see our intangible fear. Our close friends and family can see our negative patterns long before we do and when they try and tell us about them we just don't hear or don't get it. You probably know someone in your own circle of friends or family who repeats the same bad pattern over and over again with regards to work, relationships or health but you can never make them understand what they are doing wrong.

However, once we know about intangible fear or the inner gremlin, and we are willing to search deep within ourselves to root out and confront these demons, then we can begin to change them. This is not always an easy or quick process and it can be very painful in that moment of seeing our ugly truth, but only in seeing our darkness and fears can we begin to transform them.

Let fear and the gremlin be your compass

Everyone suffers from intangible fear, even highly successful people. The reason those people became successful is because they were able to keep moving ahead with their plans *in spite* of their fear. Although we tend to think of our gremlin as negative, the fact that it begins to act up in our life is actually positive. Obstacles caused by your inner gremlin occur when you are moving ahead, bettering yourself or beginning to pursue your heart's desires. This is good. The gremlin does not show up and stop you from sitting on the sofa with a bucket of chocolate, watching TV and getting fat. Similarly, the inner gremlin doesn't rear its head as you spend yet another evening or weekend at the office doing unpaid overtime.

Therefore, when the inner gremlin does make himself known to you – rejoice – because it means that you are making great efforts to improve your life and move closer to your true purpose or vocation.

In recent years my gremlin has been my bad back. Being tall, I have often suffered from lower back pain but in August 2006, a year into very busy activities to build my *Lead The Life* business, my pain became spectacularly bad. However, at the moment where the pain was at its most intense, and scary, I also had an amazing moment of clarity. I realised that up until that point I had focussed on the coaching side of my business but I had neglected to start giving talks and workshops, and that if I was to really fulfil my mission then I needed to get on with being a public speaker. After all, it was my desire to give inspirational talks that had led me to train as a coach in the first place. I wanted to be a speaker who also did one-to-one coaching not a coach who gave the occasional talk. The back pain, though horrific at times, caused me to alter my focus and get back on track with my own life-purpose.

Although my back has never been as bad as that time, my gremlin does try to bother me when I am making strides forward with my business and my writing. Another notable occurrence was the day before I was due to speak at a *Mind Body Soul* exhibition at London Olympia. This opportunity to speak was a dream come true for me. For years I had gone to similar shows, seen other people give inspiring talks and come away knowing that this is what I wanted to do. Now at last I was on the programme as a speaker and I also had my own stand at the exhibition. The day before the exhibition my gremlin swung into action and my back went into spasm. This was my worst fear and it was happening. Again, in the midst of the pain I had another moment of clarity and realised that I just needed to trust that my talk was good enough and that I didn't have to doubt my ability or get stressed by the last minute preparations. My talk contained an explanation of intangible fear and I knew that the back spasm was a manifestation of this. I wasn't going to be defeated. Sheer bloody-minded determination meant that I was able to man my exhibition stand for the weekend and my talk was a great success with over a hundred people attending.

That's the thing about the inner gremlin. You have to look it in the eye, say "I know you are trying to thwart me but I'm not going to let you," and carry on. If you can see the gremlin for what it is and keeping taking the right action then you will defeat it. Intangible fear will always be there and you can decide whether you win over it or not.

Exercise

Take some time to ponder the ways your gremlin materialises in your life. What are the clever, subtle ways that you have been hoodwinked by your gremlin?

Getting one over on your inner gremlin

You can defeat your gremlin. Your first line of defence is knowledge that the gremlin exists and that any obstacles that arise are only manifestations of your intangible fear and do not have to be real obstacles. Then I find that the best way to keep moving when fear strikes is to break everything down to really small steps. This way there is always something easy to do that will get you back on track towards your goals. When you start with small easy steps your confidence grows and before you know it you are building up exciting momentum. Then, when you reach the next scary point you can look back and see that you have already won through some challenges so it is likely that you can win again.

Knowledge can also be an effective weapon against the gremlin. Sometimes we get stuck in our plans because we genuinely do not know what to do. If your goal requires you to borrow a substantial sum of money from a bank and you have no idea how to put together a business plan then you are probably going to feel very scared and very stuck. However, there are lots of ways to learn about business plans. You can get a book on it, hire a business coach or go on a course. In fact, many of the high street banks hand out free software that takes you through the steps of putting the plan together. As you gain the required knowledge you can start to take the right action again.

Back in 2005 when I made the declaration that I was going to be a public speaker and give talks and workshops, I had no idea how to actually go about doing this. Two weeks later I bumped into a friend who had just embarked on a certificate in coaching. She sent me the details of her course and this was the springboard to me to research coaching qualifications. In the end I opted for a coaching diploma. The coaching industry in the UK is currently unregulated so there was nothing to stop me just printing out some business cards stating that I was a coach and getting on with it. However, I am so glad that I got some formal training as this gave me a framework not only on how to work with clients but also how to set up my business and go about building a coaching practice. The qualification opened up networking opportunities and also gave me ideas for the talks and workshops that I wanted to present.

Knowledge is a wonderful weapon against the gremlin but beware, the gremlin can sometimes use this against you. One manifestation of intangible fear is feeling that you just do not know enough to embark on your dreams and goals. This can lead you to taking, and paying for, course after course after course, but never actually doing what you want to do. You will need to use your wisdom to decipher whether you really need another qualification or whether you are using this as a delaying tactic to taking more tangible action towards your goals.

You may need to play along with your gremlin. One of my workshops is called *Stop Procrastinating, Start Doing* and is about deep-seated resistance and how to overcome it. Two days before I presented the workshop for the first time, sure enough I had my own fear attack and had a huge desire to crawl under a table and hide away from the world. After about half an hour of sitting fairly paralysed with fear in my office chair, achieving nothing, I decided to follow through on this wish to hide under the table so I did just that. I pulled my chair away from the desk, got down on my hands and knees, crawled underneath the desk and curled up on the floor. As soon as I did this I saw how funny and ridiculous the situation was, I laughed at myself and at my gremlin, then got out from under the desk, sat back down in my office chair and got on with my work. The gremlin will always show up when we are making good strides forwards, so we might as well have fun with it when it does!

Sometimes it feels as if we hit a brick wall with our plans. Again, this is the gremlin at work. There is always a way past the wall. You may have to burrow under it, sneak round the edge when the gremlin isn't looking or find a ladder and climb over it. You don't have to do this alone. You can enlist the help of friends or professional advisors. Or you may be able to hire someone else to take care of that part of the wall for you. Where there is a will there is most definitely a way.

Ultimately to overcome any fear, procrastination or anything else the gremlin may chuck at you, you must keep up the dialogue between your head and your heart. As long as you can keep balancing the desires and mitigating the fears of these two parties you can keep moving towards your goals and enjoy the journey. Have regular check-ins with yourself, re-focus or re-calibrate your plans whenever necessary and, if in doubt, break the tasks down into the smallest steps that you can.

Exercise

This is where you get to be a child. You are going to make a model of your inner gremlin. You can use plasticine, scrunched up paper, egg boxes, old cereal packets – anything you can find to make a representation of your gremlin. Stick together the components with glue or sellotape as best you can. Feel free to use coloured pens, pencils or paints too.

When you have finished making your gremlin you will need a black dustbin sack. Put your gremlin inside, tie up the sack, and place it on the floor. Now jump up and down on it with vigour shouting "I know who you are and you will never thwart my plans again!"

I finish my *Stop Procrastinating, Start Doing* workshop with the above exercise and the participants always find it fun and liberating. It can be daunting dealing with our darkest fears and rooting out the cause of our self-sabotage. Sometimes we can despair of our own shortcomings. However, please take faith that everyone has a gremlin and everyone has a battle going on between their head and their heart. You are no worse, or frightened or useless than anybody else. The stuff that our gremlin throws at us forces us to grow. Overcoming our obstacles enables us to reveal our greatness and very often those obstacles can be transformed into our greatest treasure.

Chapter 7 :

Change Your Unhelpful Mindset

The map is not the territory

There is a theory in the personal development world that the map is not the territory. This means that just because the map is presented in a certain way, it does not follow that the actual terrain matches the representation of the map. If ten people were given the task of mapping out a specific geographical area, they would do it in their own way, focussing on landmarks which jumped out at them and to a scale and precision of their choosing. Although the resulting ten maps would bear some similarities to the actual landscape, they would each be unique. One landscape, ten different maps.

We all have our own map that covers the journey of the past, present and future of our life, but that does not mean that it represents the truth. It is merely our version of what we think that truth is. We see life through our own specially designed spectacles, the lenses of which are made from our habits, thought patterns and rules. We see and experience the world according to our own filters. We also look into the future with these same spectacles and therefore have pre-conceived ideas about how a future event or experience may pan out for us and more often than not our predictions are fulfilled.

For example, two people, Bill and Sue, visit London for the first time. Bill is from Sheffield and had heard that people in the South of England, particularly London, are not very friendly, do not look out for each other or are always looking for an opportunity to rip off a visitor. On the train at St Pancras station he arrived with a deeply suspicious attitude and ready to do battle with anyone who may cross his path. He needed to take the London underground to get to his hotel and knowing that it was every man for himself he barged straight on to the tube train when its doors opened rather than waiting for the passengers to get off first. This caused him a few scowls from his fellow travellers. Once on the crowded train he was reluctant to move to one side and let people on and off and was therefore pushed about by the 'unfriendly' Londoners. After dinner that evening, having complained to the waiter about the high prices, he went into a pub for a pint of beer and, misunderstanding the foreign accent of the barman, was served a pint of premium Belgian larger when he only wanted the regular stuff. "Bloody rip off," he muttered as he reluctantly handed over his money.

Sue on the other hand, was very excited about visiting London as she had heard that you can meet lots of people from different cultures and that Londoners were very open, forward-thinking people. In the taxi from the airport, she had an interesting conversation with the driver about London life during the Second World War and found the concierge at her hotel very helpful on procuring theatre tickets for *Phantom of The Opera*. When she dropped her gloves in the underground she gracefully thanked the Japanese gentleman who noticed her loss and alerted her to the fallen gloves. While waiting for her cappuccino to be made in

Starbucks, she chatted with the Polish lady at the till about English versus continental European culture. Same city, two different pre-conceived ideas that led to two different experiences of the same territory.

In the last two or three years as the credit crunch occurred the prevailing viewpoint was doom and gloom and we witnessed some well-known names disappearing from the high street. However, some companies saw opportunity: Domino's Pizza expanded as people stopped paying to go out to restaurants and started to treat themselves by eating pizza at home and the cut price supermarket chains such as Lidl and Aldi flourished. Cinema attendance also increased. The version of the map that we choose to read can have a big impact on our thought processes and whether we view a particular set of circumstances as a disaster or an opportunity.

The reason I am explaining 'the map is not the territory' is summed up by Henry Ford when he said, "Whether you think you can or think you can't, you are usually right". Your mindset and what you believe to be true will determine your success, or otherwise, at achieving your goals. If this statement troubles you, then don't worry – because beliefs and mindsets can be changed whether you require a 180° change or just a bit of fine tuning. You can produce a better map for yourself. Throughout this chapter we will examine whether some of the things you believe really are true and then I will give you some ways that you can gradually change your unhelpful beliefs.

Are you 'too' limited?

When we think negatively of ourselves and doubt our capabilities the word 'too' often comes into play. I'm too old, too young, too fat, too thin, too short or too tall. When we say this it is like we are hitting ourselves with a big stick and saying "you're just not good enough". Again, just because we think these things doesn't make them true. You may think you are too far into middle age to get fit and go jogging and yet every year old age pensioners compete in and complete the London Marathon. You may think you are too young to fulfil your professional ambitions but Karren Brady became CEO of Birmingham City Football club at just twenty-three years old, and she was the wrong sex! Where there is a will, there is most definitely a way. Otherwise how could people with physical disabilities compete in the Olympics or climb mountains, how could those with illness such as Jane Tomlinson or Lance Armstrong succeed in monumental physical endurance tests and how can Sue Townsend continue to write books about Adrian Mole even though she is blind?

When you say "I'm too something or other" you are saying "I can't" and when you say "I can't" what you really mean is "I'm not willing". That is okay. Maybe you are not willing to do a certain activity but understand that you are choosing not to do it and take responsibility for this decision.

When I was writing the first draft of this book, my book coach wanted me to go at a faster pace than I was comfortable with. In my moments of feeling sorry for myself I was saying "I just can't go at this pace. I just can't do it". 'Can't' is not a very empowering state to be in. 'Can't' is a miserable state where you whimper away to yourself and anyone you can find who will stick around and listen to you. Changing 'can't' to 'not willing' is empowering. I'm not willing to find twelve hours a week to write. I'm not willing to work when my back, neck and shoulders are hurting. I'm not willing to give up much needed relaxation time. 'Not willing' is empowering because it gives you choice. You are

92

stating that you are not willing to do something or other and then you can ask yourself "what am I willing to do?" In the case of my writing I was willing to do between eight and ten hours a week. And I was willing to switch to writing by hand when it got painful to use the computer and so work continued on the first draft. I was much happier, my body was much happier and hopefully you are happier because you get to read the fruits of these labours!

Exercise

What do you tell yourself that you can't do? Perhaps you are too old, young, rich or poor etc. Instead of using the word 'can't' admit to yourself that you are simply not willing to do it. Then ask yourself what you are willing to do.

It ain't necessarily so

To quote George and Ira Gershwin, it ain't necessarily so. Just because you believe it does not make it true. Also, just because it may have been true earlier in your life, that doesn't mean that this belief applies to today.

Many of our beliefs are formed when we are young and are often handed to us by an older person in authority such as parent or teacher. For example, William was a quieter and more reflective child than Frank. He was soon labelled by his parents as 'the quiet one'. William kept this identity all the way through school and his parents always told his teachers that he was the quiet one. Despite wishing to act in the school play or sing solo in the choir William never put himself forward for this because he was too quiet (there's the 'too' again). This continued into his adult life and for many years he wanted to volunteer to give talks and presentations at work but he always felt that he could not do this because only people who are outspoken could possibly hold the attention of an audience. However, as part of his work as a biologist he developed an expertise in the changes to water supplies caused by urbanisation and eventually plucked up the courage to give a talk at conference. Even though he was nervous and a little bit stilted at the start of the talk, as he got going his passion and detailed knowledge of the subject shone through and many people told him afterwards that his talk was very interesting and asked him further questions on the topic. This surprised him because he had never seen himself as outgoing and had always concluded that he had nothing interesting to say.

Our beliefs that we acquired in childhood can plague us through our adult life. Ivor found it difficult to join in with games with other children. As he became an adult this manifested in him finding it hard to form trusting work relationships and throughout his career he was labelled as 'not a team player'. After a while if he changed job or moved to a new department he stopped expecting that he would fit in to the team and was very defensive around his colleagues and did not share information with them that he should have. He always felt that he needed to keep something to himself in case he needed to use it against people or keep it in reserve if someone tried to get one over him. This behaviour spilled over in to his personal life; he only had one or two close friends and he sometimes experienced difficult moments in those friendships. When he split up with his long-term girlfriend he felt very alone. Not being allowed to join in with the games at school had brought him to a very lonely and depressing place. He desperately wanted to increase his circle of friendships and eventually to meet another woman. He thought about joining a club or taking up a hobby or evening class but he just assumed that he couldn't fit in with the people there and they wouldn't want him to join their group, so what was the point of putting himself through that again?

When Ivor started having coaching with me, I noticed how much he always mentioned 'not fitting in', 'doesn't get on with people, 'not good in teams'. I talked to him about beliefs and then I asked him to think back to when he first experienced this feeling of 'not fitting in' and 'not being allowed to join in the game'. He reeled off a list of occasions in his adult life when this had been the case and then moved back in time to similar situations at college. Then he paused and told me about a time at junior school when some boys had not let him join in a ball game they were playing during the lunch break at school.

"Why do you think they might have stopped you?" I asked.

"I had my arm in a sling," he replied.

"Really, why was that?" I asked

"I'd been walking a neighbour's dog and it had seen another dog, leapt to run after it and pulled me over. I dislocated my shoulder."

"Do you think it was anything to do with your arm being in a sling that they didn't let you play?' I asked.

"Maybe," he said.

I asked him to look at that situation with adult eyes – and the benefit of life. What were his thoughts on it?

"Maybe they didn't want me to hurt myself," he replied. "Come to think of it, my Mum had told a couple of my mates that they mustn't play rough games with me in case I made my shoulder worse. I think I had ripped the muscle quite badly."

"So is it possible that they stopped you from playing with them, not because they didn't want you to play, but because they didn't want to hurt you or get in trouble with your mum?"

He nodded and then added, "And for the last twenty five years I have thought that no-one wanted to play with me!"

As be began to see that his beliefs around 'not fitting in' were no longer true this then gave him the freedom to approach work and social situations differently.

Even though Ivor had the major revelation about the real reasons why he was not included in the ball game at junior school, over the next couple of appointments with me he said that he still found it hard to shake the belief that he did not fit in and that he couldn't work well with other people. When we are bogged down over a long period of time with a negative mindset we tend to apply it in a blanket way saying things like "No-one likes me" or "Everybody ignores me" or "I can never get this right". Sweeping generalist words such as 'everyone', 'no-one', 'never' or 'always' creep into our thoughts and conversations and we think the belief is true all of the time even if daily events prove otherwise. In Ivor's case I pointed out that he and I had built a good relationship and were working very well together so in this particular instance his belief of not being able to work well with people simply wasn't valid. As his homework, I set Ivor the challenge of finding situations where his belief was not true. For example; if there was in instance at work where he successfully gave or received help from a colleague then that was an instance where the belief wasn't true. If a passer-by asked him for directions or help then that was an opportunity for him to see the belief wasn't true. Likewise; if he needed to ask someone else for help then that would be an opportunity for the belief not to be true. In fact, I challenged him to approach people in the street and ask directions or the time just to prove to himself that people were willing to work with him. In this way he gradually proved to himself that he did have a valid contribution to make in work as well as personal relationships and slowly he accepted the evidence that people were willing to interact with him.

It is easier to change a belief when you can see some evidence that it is no longer true or is not true in all situations.

How to change unhelpful beliefs

If beliefs are just thoughts and the ones that limit us tend to be recurring negative cycles, then one way to change these thought patterns is to intercept them and make the cycle more positive. The best way to create a positive thought is to take the negative statement and then change it to a positive opposite. See the table on the next page for some examples:

Negative Limiting Belief	Replace With Positive Opposite
'I'm no good at maths.'	'I am excellent at maths.' 'I am very confident with numbers.'
'I find it hard to make friends.'	'I am outstanding at making friends and people are very glad to get to know me.'
'I'm crap at sales calls.'	'I am excellent at making sales calls and get customers easily.'
'I'm too old to begin a new career.'	'I am just at the right age to start something new and my previous experience is a wonderful asset to my new endeavour.'
'I can't spell.'	'I am very talented at spelling.'
'I'm a terrible writer.'	'I am a wonderful writer and regularly produce beautifully written prose'

Notice the pattern in the positive opposites.

They are positive and can have an extra positive outcome on the end. For example: I am very gifted at marketing *and* my business is flourishing.

They are present tense i.e. I have, I can, I am, even though these statements might not be true – yet.

They are powerful. They don't just say 'I am good at writing', they go one-step further and say 'I am outstanding at writing.' You can have fun making these statements powerfully outrageous.

Once you have your positive, powerful opposite statement, you can then catch the negative thought as it occurs. As you think the same old negative thought, imagine the word 'delete' flashing across your mind and then replace it with your now positive, powerful opposite thought. Eventually, you will begin to see evidence that your new thought just might be true. Every time you make that thought you will feel empowered, excited and your life state will start to shift because you are no longer stuck in the negative cycle.

Exercise – Rant To Rave

You are going to come up with your own positive opposite statements in an exercise I like to call Rant To Rave.

Take a sheet of paper and start writing all your negative rants about how crap you are, how you can't do X, Y or Z and throw in as many 'too' statements as your inner gremlin wants. Let all your pessimistic rubbish come up and out.

Now take each of those statements and create a powerful positive, present tense opposite from them. These powerful positive statements will give you a tailor made set of affirmations designed especially for you.

If you really want to start believing the positive opposite statements then take a few minutes each day and write down one your positive statements five times. As you do this you will probably feel a lot of negative stuff boiling up again about how the statement can't possibly be true and you will probably stir up some poisonous feelings. Persist in writing out your positive statement five times and then write down and capture all the negative outpourings. Just as you did before, take this load of negative proclamations and make more powerful, positive, present tense opposite statements from them. This will give you even more tailor made affirmations.

Over the course of a few days, this layering process of building affirmations from your rants means that you are likely to drill down to the real bedrock fear and bad belief which is really at the foundation of why you are feeling negatively about yourself. It is good to be conscious of this fundamental fear or bad belief because when you are aware of what it really is then you can change it. Our negative thoughts and beliefs are often the reason we procrastinate, fail and start a project which is dear to our hearts or fail to continue with it when we meet an obstacle.

Exercise – Your Fairy Godmother

Choose one of your positive statements that you have created from a bedrock or foundation bad belief – or one that feels very pertinent to you. Imagine that your Fairy Godmother has arrived and has granted this positive statement as a wish. From this moment onwards your positive statement is absolutely true. As it is true then the previous bad belief is no longer an issue to you. Now that this obstacle has been removed what ideas do you have in taking action towards your goals? What can you go and easily do now?

On a recent workshop, one of the participants was sceptical about the power of using positive opposite statements to change beliefs. He said that he was really bad at doing DIY so, if he made some present tense, positive statement about how great he was at plumbing, would I let him into my house to put in a new bath and shower. I laughed and said I wouldn't, but I added that if he was serious about changing his mindset about his DIY capabilities then in replacing his negative thought with the positive statement he might find that he gets better at small jobs such as changing a plug, painting a room or assembling a set of shelves. Over time through working at the positive thoughts and taking consistent action to improve and learn new DIY skills he might one day find that he could re-plumb a bathroom. Changing your mindset and seeing proof of a better outcome takes time, you need to chip away at it bit by bit and you also need wisdom and patience. Someone else in the workshop asked whether we need to be good at everything. No, I replied. I told them that I'm also very bad at DIY but I am accepting of this because I am very good at earning enough money to pay someone else to do those jobs. It is okay to accept your short-comings. You do not have to be good at everything, but if a bad mindset or belief or lack of skill is holding you back, causing you pain or making you miserable in any way then please remember that you have the power within you to change it.

Chapter 8:

Time And Money

My observations when either attending or giving personal development workshops is that the two big obstacles that people perceive as a barrier to getting on with the life they really want are time and money. A common comment is that achieving your dream is possible but it would be hell of a lot easier if you won the lottery first.

Some thoughts on time

Not having enough time seems to be a universal predicament especially in modern life. While the last one hundred years has given us enormous strides forward in terms of technology and labour saving devices, the promised leisure time that such advancements were supposed to bring have not materialised and instead we just demand more of ourselves. Technology such as email, the internet or mobile phones which were supposed to make business life easier, have in fact, added a burden of information on us and we are expected to respond quickly to these requests for communication. As women have taken up roles within the workplace, in general they haven't relinquished family responsibilities so this just adds to the burden of activity that each family member is required to undertake. Activities can take longer than they used to, for example, the time taken to get to work because we tend to travel further than we used to and the roads have more traffic, or train services seem to deteriorate rather than improve.

Managing time is a constant balancing act and very few people feel that they have enough of it. However, some manage to get more done than others, yet we all have the same twenty-four hour day to contend with. How can you become more efficient in the time you have available?

Sometimes there is an inverse relationship between time and money. This means that if you throw some money at a problem you can reduce the time you personally need to spend on solving it. A few years ago when I was juggling work as an IT consultant with building my personal development business, I identified two items that I needed to spend money on in order to save time. The first was to buy a dishwasher and the second was to have a cleaner. I calculated that this would save me four hours a week in domestic activity which would free me up to either spend more time on my business or take much needed time to rest and relax. This made a huge difference to the juggling act between my day job and my business, and my flat became a more pleasant environment in which to work! Getting a Blackberry also made it easier to manage my business email and meant that I no longer needed to come home from my day job only to plonk myself in front of my computer and attend to emails. Instead I had already dealt with them on the train home.

It is not always about time, even though you think it is. It is very easy to squander time. When I first started to write I wrongly assumed that I needed huge swathes of time to sit around and 'be creative'. However, in reality it only takes me about ten minutes to handwrite one page of a manuscript or about half an hour to write 300-400 words on a computer. Writing, therefore, doesn't have to take all day. It can be done in small pockets of time in and around daily life. Yesterday I was stuck on a train for an hour because it had a fault. Eventually I decided to cease huffing and puffing with irritation about the delay and stop wasting time playing games on my Blackberry. Instead, I pulled out my pad and wrote two pages of this manuscript. In the past I have written one or two pages before going to work and I have also written at lunchtimes while in a café waiting for my food to arrive. It does not have to be about having more time; instead you need to learn to use the time that you do have.

Having too much time can be counterproductive to moving forward with your dreams. Two years ago Ray was made redundant as an IT Support Manager. He decided not to look for another job but to take his redundancy money and set up a business selling antiques over the internet. In his last few days of IT work he was very excited about his plans and as he left the office on Friday afternoon for the very last time he couldn't wait to get started on them. However, when his first Monday morning of freedom dawned, he decided to take it easy for a few days and to enjoy not having to get up and work. Two things happened. Firstly, without his former work colleagues egging him on and encouraging him, he became very daunted and scared about the prospect of setting up his business and the costs and investments involved. He felt very lonely and wasn't sure whether he could pull off his intended undertaking. Secondly, he got very comfy in not having a rigid work routine. He enjoyed getting up later, having time for a leisurely breakfast with the newspaper, doing the crossword and getting on with some DIY jobs around the house. He also enjoyed taking time to meet friends for lunch and going to the cinema in the afternoon when the ticket prices were cheaper. He did start playing around with websites and making contacts with a couple of local antique shops, but he never really got his idea off the ground. Ten months later his redundancy money was running low and he ended up taking another job in IT. He buried his business idea and when people asked him about it he just shrugged and said it didn't work out.

It is easy to fall in to Ray's trap. If you don't believe me, take a week off work and see how much action you really get done towards your dreams and goals.

If Ray had built the foundations of his business while still working in a day job, then he may have had a more disciplined approach to it. He would have still had the safety net of his salary and the social interaction and encouragement from his colleagues. He also would have made better use of his time and would have been eager to complete the activities towards his business. Then he could have made a more gradual and less scary transition from IT to relying on his business for his income. Or, he could have decided to keep his IT work and just do the business on the side. This may have been a fulfilling combination for him.

Time management is in your head

The secret to time management is in your head, it is about decisions and choices. *You* need to decide how your time is spent and take the control in situations where others want to take up *your* time. There is a theory called Parkinson's Law which states the amount of time required to perform a task will expand to the amount of time available for it. Therefore, if you have to get a proposal document written by next Friday you may do a little bit of thinking and planning on it now. However, you are unlikely to complete it until Friday itself, probably with most of the work going into it on Thursday. If, however, you hear that your competitors are going to be turning in their documents on Wednesday you will probably find that you can get yours done by that day too. The task takes up the amount of time that we plan to spend on it.

We can therefore use Parkinson's Law to our advantage. You can decide how long a task will take and when you will get it finished. You can determine to return five phone calls before your twelve o'clock meeting or get through your emails by three o'clock or to spend two hours preparing a presentation. When we make a conscious decision about how much time to give to a task there is more chance that we will get it done in that time frame than if we just drift along without a plan.

Time management is also about communication. You need to constantly communicate your time parameters to others. For example, at work if you have to return a phone call you can say "I've five minutes now before my next meeting, can we cover it quickly during this time or do we need to book an appointment?" If you are managing someone at work who always bothers you with trivial questions you can say "Hi John, I am busy at the moment. Is your question more than an eight out of ten in terms of importance? If not, save it up with any other questions and we'll sit down at four o'clock and go through them." You can also use these techniques in your personal life. If you need to phone Auntie Mary and thank her for the Christmas present she sent you and she usually talks at you for at least an hour about nothing in particular then you can start your conversation with "Hi Auntie Mary, I have a friend coming round in ten minutes but I just wanted to give you a quick call and say thank you for the reindeer-patterned pyjamas that you sent me." Auntie Mary is happy because you've phoned her and you are happy because you get off the phone in a lot quicker time than normal. When you lay down time boundaries to other people, more often than not they will respect them.

Another fundamental law of time management is that an activity will either take you closer to your goals or away from them. It's that simple – you can use this law to decide whether or not to perform an activity or to prioritise which activity will take you closest to your goals. Of course, to get the most from this law you need to know what your goals are. Then you can make better decisions about how to organise your time.

Where are your time blockages?

In chapter four we looked at what you would need to lose or let go of in order to achieve your dreams. Go back to this chapter and review the list of losses that you wrote down. When you think about the time involved with these items does it motivate you to let go of them?

Also, think about where the bottlenecks in your day occur when time suddenly disappears. One of my clients, Julia, had made the jump to building a freelance graphic design business rather than working as an employee for someone else. However, without the structure and discipline of having to clock in at the office at a prescribed time she was struggling to get started on her work early enough in the day at her home office. I asked her at what time she wanted to begin her work day and she replied nine o'clock. Then I asked her how much time she needed to get up, shower and have breakfast before starting work. She replied that she needed an hour and a half in total because she liked to go out for a walk to get some exercise and fresh air before getting busy with work and that she picked up a cappuccino from a local café on the way back. That meant that she needed to be getting up at 7.30am. I asked her how much sleep she needed. When she replied that she preferred to have eight hours we calculated that she needed to be tucked up in bed by 11.30pm. Then I asked her how much time she needed to get ready for bed. She replied that it took her quite a long time. She liked to do the washing up, fold up any laundry, do a few stretches then go through her skincare routine. She realised that all of that took about an hour which meant that she needed to stop whatever she was doing at 10.30pm and get started on her going to bed routine. This was a revelation for Julia. She hadn't recognised that her going to bed routine was a time blockage because she had been starting it at her bed time of 11.30pm. Consequently she was not getting to bed until after midnight and then struggling to get up in time to start work at 9am.

Going to bed early enough is a vital part of time management and sometimes it is necessary to look at the factors that prevent that happening. Watching television and surfing the internet are major time-eaters and can frequently lead to going to bed later than intended. One way around this is to make sure you do not eat dinner in front of the television as then you are more likely to stay in front of it for the remainder of the evening. Another way to manage television viewing is to decide in advance which programmes you would like to watch and either tune-in just for that programme or record it and watch it at a time that suits. This takes up less time than channel surfing and getting drawn in to something that you weren't intending to watch. Alternatively you could get rid of your television or unplug all of the cables between your television and the various devices it is attached to and put them in a cupboard in a different room. You are less likely to spend time reconnecting the TV to watch nothing in particular.

Sometimes a time blockage occurs because you are trying to do an activity at the wrong time of day. Sam ran a small firm of financial advisors and once a week liked to take off early and spend a few hours doing voluntary work at a local hospice. The hospice needed him from 3pm but he often found it stressful to get away from the office at 2.30pm because the afternoon had got underway and he was often drawn into meetings and discussions with his staff. When we analysed this blockage Sam realised that if he left the office at lunchtime then his departure was much smoother as everyone was at lunch and problems needing his attention had not yet arisen. It was easier for him to leave the office at 1.30pm than at 2.30pm to keep his commitment of arriving at the hospice by 3pm. He used the extra hour away from his desk to return phone calls from the morning and also take a few minutes and go for a much needed walk.

Exercise

What are your time blockages and what logistical solutions could you put in place to overcome them?

Time saving tips to spend less time at work

You can use these tips to become more efficient at work and then you will have more time to spend on your dreams. You can also apply these tips to the time you spend building your personal goals. The tips will help save you small pockets of time but they will not work miracles. If you are overworked and understaffed then you may need to come up with other solutions.

Make a realistic daily to-do list

Human beings respond better to success than to failure. Therefore, only put on your daily to-do list what you can realistically hope to finish. There is nothing more satisfying than ticking your way all the way through a list. Keep the list shorter rather than longer and then if you have time left at the end of the day you can do one or two additional tasks and feel even better about your achievements. When you are deciding in which order to do the tasks, group like tasks together. For example, make phone calls in one batch or attend to emails in one session. Use Parkinson's Law and decide how long you want the tasks to take.

Managing your overall to-do list

You probably have far more things on your plate than just what you place on a daily to-do list. If you have a lot of projects on the go or a lot of demands landing on you, then it is very easy to feel overwhelmed, the stress of which will not help you to work effectively. To manage all these things and decide on the best priority go through the following exercise: take a sheet of paper, turn it so that it is landscape and draw two lines down it to make three columns of equal width. At the top of the first column write the heading *Urgent and Important.* Above the second column write the heading *Important but Not Urgent* and above the third column write *Urgent but Not Important.* Now go through each of the pieces of work that you have to do and tasks that must get done and write them down in the appropriate column.

You will find that most of your tasks will end up in the first two columns. The tasks in the first column, *Urgent and Important*, usually have a deadline within the next few days. Decide which of these has the highest priority and put its component parts on your to-do list for today.

The items in the second column, *Important but not Urgent*, tend to be of a more maintenance or housekeeping nature. If you run your own business then marketing and bookkeeping activities tend to fall into this category. If you take care of them on a regular basis then they don't end up in the first column as an urgent task. You may like to organise your week whereby you spend an allotted period of time doing the tasks from this column so that you always stay on top of them. For example, you could spend Friday afternoon tidying up your email Inbox or doing much needed filing.

Hopefully you will not have any items in the third column. If a task is urgent but not important then why are you doing it? Does this task really need to be done or can you delegate it to someone else?

Take a few minutes to plan your day, week or month
You can save time by spending just a few minutes to plan out your day, week or longer periods of time. Some people like to spend time first thing in the morning to plan, others like to do it at the end of the day for the following day. Alternatively you can take a few minutes on a Sunday night or Monday morning to map out the shape of your week. I quite like spending a few minutes of reflection last thing on a Friday afternoon to decide on the priorities for the next week. When you do your planning use Parkinson's Law to determine how much time you want to spend on each activity. Don't forget to constantly communicate

the parameters of your plan to other people so that they don't mess up your productivity.

Dealing with emergencies

No matter how well you have planned out your day, unforeseen events will occur. When an emergency lands, either by phone or by email it is tempting to go straight in to headless chicken mode, run around and deal with the crisis there and then, totally forgetting what you were supposed to be working on. In fact, successfully fire-fighting an emergency can give you quite a buzz and it can be good to be the hero and solve the issues as they come up. The only problem with this approach is that if you do it too often you never actually achieve your own goals or objectives. Days, weeks or months can go by and the work you are supposed to be doing doesn't get done.

Next time an unforeseen emergency lands on you, do not react immediately. Instead, tell the person that you just need to spend a few moments thinking about the situation and that you will get back to them in ten minutes. Now step away from the phone or computer and think – does this situation really have to be dealt with immediately? Can you continue with what you were doing and then respond to it later in the day or tomorrow? Can you delegate it to someone else? Just because the person who contacted you thinks it is an emergency is it *your* emergency? Do you have to do anything about it at all? When you have collected your thoughts then phone the person back and tell them your plan. Nine times out of ten they will be satisfied with your response.

In this way you have taken control of the situation and made a decision about how you will let it affect your time. Occasionally you will be faced with a real emergency where you have to drop everything and deal with it, but mostly it can be dealt with at a time which suits you and causes the least interruption to your existing work.

Email

Email has become a huge time eater in modern office life for two reasons: firstly, we get too many of them because we are copied on emails which really aren't that important and secondly, because we tend to leave email running all day long and respond to it every time we see a new one arrive. If email is running on your computer all the time then you are constantly interrupted by it. The interruption is not just the time that it takes you to read the new email but also the time it takes you to get back into your train of thought of what you were originally working on.

Train yourself to only look at emails at certain times of the day such as 9am, 12pm, and 3pm or at a time interval which is suitable for you. Then in your daily planning allocate time at those specified intervals to deal with the email. Anything that takes less than two minutes to deal with can be done immediately. Tasks that will take longer can be planned in to your day for later on or for the following day. Again, just like the to-do list, you can give some thought as to whether each email is *important and urgent*, *important but not urgent* or *urgent but not important*; then you can assign it an appropriate priority.

Like all matters relating to time management, communication is important when dealing with email only at specified times. You can let people know when you will respond to emails by putting the times on an out-of-office auto responder or make it generally known to your colleagues when you look at email. When I was doing some writing a couple of years ago, I told all my clients that I would not look at email until late afternoon so they were primed not to expect an immediate response from me.

Phones

Phones, like email, can constantly interrupt us and hijack our daily plan. Depending on the nature of your work you may be able to let the phone go to voicemail. Then you can finish off what you were doing and deal with the call later. If your mobile phone is always ringing then also consider having a voicemail response which states the specific times that you check messages and that you will return phone calls at those times. Again, communicate when you speak to the caller that you can deal with the query straightaway if it is quick, otherwise you would like to reschedule a time to have a more in-depth conversation with them.

Meetings

Meetings can also be big time eaters which prevent actual work from being done. Typically, when we are arranging a meeting we book a meeting room for an hour and block out this time span in our diary. Why not use Parkinson's Law and determine to get the meeting done in forty-five minutes? If you have back to back meetings then you can use the time you have saved in between them to make phone calls or check your email.

Communicate at the start of the meeting when it will finish and always have an agenda. Do not allow *Any Other Business* at the end of the agenda. Instead get all the participants to email you with any issues they have before hand. Then you can allocate time to them and if there are too many issues you can bump those with a lower priority to another time slot.

Establish your peak time

There are probably times of the day when you can really power through your work and other times when you are sluggish and you don't seem to get much done. If you don't know when you are at your peak then conduct a time and motion study on yourself; over a period of two days write down every activity that you do and whether you feel you are at low, medium or high energy. Notice the pattern of where your high or peak energy occurs and then use this to your advantage. Plan important activities into this time and use less peak time for meetings, returning phone calls or checking emails. I am at my best between 9am and 1pm and then again between 5pm and 7pm. During these time slots I like to keep interruptions to a minimum and will communicate that accordingly.

Final thoughts on time

It is easier to work with time than against it. Going against time is a losing battle. Occasionally time management is realising that you just don't have time for a specific activity at the moment. Sometimes it is easier to accept this fact than try and shoehorn too many things in to your life. Notice that I said that it might not fit *at the moment*. That doesn't mean that you will never get to an activity it just means that now is not the best time. If you are in this predicament then go back to chapter four and have a think about what, eventually, you might be able to let go of that will free up the much needed time that you need.

Sometimes we need time to recover from one set of activities before launching into another. Time for rest and relaxation is also important. I love *Lord of the Rings* by J.R.R Tolkien. Every time that I read the book I am struck by the fact that when, in the *Fellowship of the Ring*, the hobbits reach Elrond's house, they spend a few weeks there recuperating from the first stage of the journey. Then time is spent summoning interested parties to discuss what to do with the ring. Only when the time is right, and Frodo is fully recovered, do they set off on the next stage of the journey. In what ways do you need to recuperate and how can you use your wisdom to decide when the time is right to proceed with the next stage of your journey?

Money wisdom

Money is a very taboo subject. You probably know more about your friends' sex lives than you know about how much they earn and how they manage their bank balance. Very early on in my personal development journey I went to a seminar where one of the exercises was to stand up with our wallets in one hand while pointing at it with the other hand, saying "I'm not going to let you be the reason I can't achieve my dreams." It was a very powerful exercise in making the choice to step beyond the constraints of money.

In this section I am going to present to you some of the lessons I have learnt over the years about attitudes to money. I'm not going to teach you how to invest it, nor how to get rich and this is not a lesson on generating abundance. There are plenty of other books and seminars available on all of these topics. I'm simply going to present you with a few thoughts. You can follow them up or discount them at your will.

You can't get rich by counting your neighbours wealth

It is easy to be envious of other people's financial good fortune but no amount of jealousy or resentment of their wealth is going to improve your own financial position. In fact, this attitude is likely to ensure that you stay dissatisfied with your own finances. The energy that you are wasting counting someone else's wealth could be better spent on accepting where you are at and doing what you can to change it. If you want to be intensely interested in someone else's money then at least do so in a way that you can learn from them.

I was very lucky to come across personal development masters like Jim Rohn in my twenties. One of the early lessons that I learnt from Jim is that you are paid what you are worth to the market which can sometimes be a harsh realisation. It can be frustrating to think that a nurse, a policeman or a teacher is not worth as much as an investment banker, a chief exec or an IT consultant. But on purely financial terms they are not. The market is not willing to pay a nurse as much as a bond trader. If a nurse wants to earn more money she has to make some tough decisions about her career or learn to make money from other sources.

Notice that I used the word 'learn' in the last sentence. To increase your worth to the market you usually need to learn a new skill. If I want to sell more books then I have to learn about book marketing. If you want more customers then you may need to learn better sales techniques. If you want to get promoted to a higher pay scale then you need to learn how to manage people. If you want to jump on the latest high paying IT craze then you will need to learn about the technology behind it. If you want a better paid job then you will need to learn how to write a CV which makes the best of your current skills and experience. If you want to have a comfortable pension when you are older then you will need to learn some long-term investment techniques.

One of my observations of office life is that some people think they are entitled to a pay rise purely because they have worked for a company for a certain number of years. If the pay rise doesn't happen or it isn't as big as they had wished then you will hear them moan, "I've worked for this company all this time and this is all I got." Again, you get paid what you are worth in the market and if long service does not make you worth more in your current employment then you need to change jobs to get a decent pay hike. Companies often bring in a newcomer on a higher salary than their existing staff so maybe it's time to be that newcomer somewhere else. To increase your worth to the market and get that new job you will need to have the courage to make the move, the skill of giving a great interview and the focus and tenacity to find the best opportunity for you.

If the money isn't great where you work but everything else is a good arrangement because, for example, it is close to home or you don't have to work long hours or you have a lot of freedom or flexibility, then it may be worth staying put, especially if you are going to start taking action towards your dreams. If you are on a good number at work then quit moaning about the money and put your energy in to more constructive activities. In fact, what I'm trying to say throughout this section on money is quit moaning about it and do something more constructive instead!

Being unhappy can be expensive

Many a time in coaching I have heard clients weigh up whether to continue in a well-paid job that they are not passionate about, or change careers to something they are more interested in, but which might not be as lucrative. When assessing whether you can live on less money you need to take into account how much cash you spend because you are unhappy. If we are stressed or unhappy we tend to spend more on retail therapy to make us feel better or other items of self care to help ease the symptoms of our stress. If we are really depressed by our situation we may also be shelling out on counselling or therapy which are not cheap activities.

Heather was deciding whether to keep her job, and its comfortable salary, as an IT project manager or to take a lower paid, but more fulfilling role training underprivileged children how to make the most of their computer skills. The training role would require Heather to take a 15% pay cut and this worried her. She reflected on the cost of her unhappiness and confessed to a recent purchase of yet another pair of £200 boots and also said that she spends up to £150 a month on acupuncture to deal with her stress related neck and shoulder pains. I asked her if she wasn't paying to manage and medicate her stress could she afford the pay cut to do a job which she would really enjoy. She nodded and decided to take the plunge and say yes to the training opportunity.

Exercise

What are you spending on purely because you are fed up at work? Could you save some or all of this money and either invest it in achieving your dreams or downsize to a more fulfilling life?

Dealing with time and money is often a difficult balancing act. However, it is easier to prioritise in both of these areas if you know what you really want for your life and you are determined to take the right actions to get it!

Chapter 9:

Motivation For Continuing

We are nearing the end of the book now. If you have done the exercises then you have defined what you want from your life and figured out what would make it more fulfilling. This might mean a wholesale career change or maybe you just need to make more effort to do activities which you enjoy. You have thought about what you would need to gain in your current life and more profoundly about what you need to let go of. Then you translated achieving these gains and losses in to some action steps you can start to take right now, while still fulfilling your current responsibilities. In chapter six and seven you learnt about what might arise to thwart your efforts to create a better life for yourself and how you can continue in spite of them, safe in the knowledge that the appearance of these obstacles mean that you are on the right track. Finally, in the last chapter you learned some time management tips so that you can spend less time at work and more time taking action towards your dreams. I also suggested to you, that it is up to you whether you let lack of time or money be an obstacle to you. If you skipped over the exercises in each chapter, remember that at any time you can go back and do them.

You are all set and ready to continue on your journey. In this final chapter I want to share some more hints and tips that will help you to stick with your journey and have faith in yourself.

Riding the ups and downs

You will have times when you are surging ahead on your journey towards achieving your dreams, and you will have times when you feel like you are going backwards, when everything else takes over and you do nothing towards your dreams. Sometimes, you will hit obstacles and sometimes these obstacles will feel too big to surmount. Whatever happens, just accept what is going on as a phase in your journey and keep moving forwards. Keep taking one step at a time. If your activity has stopped, then start it again. If you meet an obstacle then do one thing towards getting over it, or round it or go via a different route. If you keep taking one step after another you will arrive somewhere. If you stop and let the obstacles or your inner gremlin win then you are going to spend a long time standing in a place that you don't like.

Every obstacle, backslide or difficult situation also carries with it a blessing. It might not feel like it at the time, but it does! Sometimes you may have to dig deep inside and muster strength you didn't know you had to find that blessing. If you can do this, even a bad situation or a defeat can give you positive value and a learning experience which will help you to fortify your strength for the journey ahead. It might be that you have not achieved your dreams yet because your life isn't ready or isn't strong enough yet. However, if you face and tackle each difficulty as they arise, then you are forging yourself into a bigger, stronger person. The obstacle is giving you the opportunity to do this. A sword is made by putting a sheet of iron into a furnace and then it is repeatedly bashed with a hammer until it is the exact right shape and cut. Then the sword is ready to go on and win victory. It is the same with your life. It may hurt to face the furnace and take the repeated blows from the hammer but if you keep the end point in sight then you will see that this treatment is absolutely necessary and without it you would not reach your goals.

When success arrives, acknowledge and celebrate it. Set yourself small and large milestones and enjoy making it to each one. After a while you will look back and be amazed at how far you have come and how, what once seemed impossible, is now accomplished. Take pride in that fact you have got started on your dreams and are continuing with them.

Exercise

This is a wonderful exercise to help you build self recognition of your achievements and to reward them. You can use it for rewards when you reach big or small milestones. Decide on the reward and then say the following to yourself:

I, [your name] am rewarding myself with [the reward] because I have [your achievements].

For example:

I, Mary Blyth, am rewarding myself with this beautiful silk scarf because today I got my first customer.

I, John Pearce, am rewarding myself with these new running shoes because I ran ten kilometres in fifty minutes today.

I, Elizabeth McCall, am rewarding myself with this cappuccino and chocolate cake because I made that scary phone call today.

Please note the three components of the phrase. You are naming yourself, you are specifying your reward and then articulating the achievement. If you do this consistently for three months for small and large achievements you will notice a significant increase in your self belief and self confidence.

I've said it before, and I will say it again – it doesn't matter how long it takes to achieve your goals, what matters is that you start taking action towards them and that you continue to take action at a pace which is manageable to you. It took me eleven years between being inspired by seeing Jim Rohn at his seminars to giving my own personal development talk and then another three years after that before I did a workshop in front of a paying audience. It was ten years ago that I started writing a novel, a book which is yet to be published. It doesn't matter how long it takes – it just matters that you do what you have to do. It is better to try, even if you subsequently fail, than to never make it to the starting blocks and lead a life of regret.

Along with patience comes kindness. In order to be patient with yourself as you reach your dreams you also have to be kind to yourself. You are not going to get everything right on day one. It can be painful when you discover that there are vital skills that you do not have and it can sometimes feel uncomfortable when you set about learning them. Find ways to be kind to yourself, to reward progress on incremental steps and to celebrate each small success long the way.

Beware of dream bashers

Although it is good to seek support and not go it completely alone when working towards your dreams, you do have to be careful who you share them with. Some people, either wittingly or unwittingly, will stamp all over your dreams the moment you utter them. As you excitedly explain your new plans you might get a grumpy and un-thought out comment like: "How are you going to sell that?" or "You won't make much money doing that" or "What does your wife/husband think about you giving up a secure job?"

These comments can be wounding and may appeal to your inner gremlin who will work very hard on nurturing that seed of doubt until you yourself think that maybe the dream basher is right and it was foolish of you to think you even had a chance of making a go of your plans.

People may put you down with their comments for a variety of reasons. Parents, for example, worry about your security and as much as they want you to be happy they also want you to play it safe so that you can make your mortgage payments every month. Their negativity comes from love. Others may be negative because deep down they are jealous of your get-up-and-go and wish they had the courage to sort out their own lives for the better. You may also come up against negativity from a close friend or relative because they are worried that the status quo in the relationship between the two of you is about to change. Perhaps the two of you have been happily jogging along together moaning about what ails you in life and now that you are starting to make changes to cure these areas of dissatisfaction, they will no longer have you as a companion in that particular rut.

On the whole these negative responses are not vindictive, though occasionally they might be; they come from love and from the person's concern either for you or themselves. Like any other attack from the inner gremlin, see this negativity as a sign that you are moving in a positive direction. Try and understand that the comments come from that person's insecurity and do your best not to let it add to yours. Thank them for their thoughts and then determine to discuss your plans with more supportive company or with someone whose opinion you trust and respect. Also remember that your parents, partner and friends may not be experts in the field of your particular dream so their opinion may not count for much anyway.

If your dreams or goals lie in the realm of your creativity also be wary of sharing your creative ideas too much, too soon, even in supportive company. When your idea is embryonic you need to nurture it yourself. Someone else's thoughts too early on may not be helpful to you and will come with that person's agenda and how they themselves would develop the idea. It is not their creative idea – it is yours and it needs to grow the way that *your* soul intends it. You can share that you have an idea for a novel, screenplay, musical or whatever it is but do not discuss the details of it until you have fleshed it out yourself and you have made the decision to pursue the idea.

Take care of your health

Working towards your dreams can be hard work and when you are fitting the action required around your existing responsibilities it can lead to a busy life. Do not neglect your health as you do this. If your health fails then you won't be able to do anything, neither your day job nor your dreams. Whilst you need to recognise when your inner gremlin is throwing a health matter at you to stop your progress, you also need the wisdom to take appropriate action to heal yourself as well as find a way to continue with your dreams.

As I mentioned earlier, there is a blessing in every obstacle. I have had various forms of back pain over the past few years and I have now developed a very close relationship with my back. When I am taking on too much, it lets me know so I now use it as a prioritising tool. If when I think about a particular project or task I can feel my back muscles tighten then I know that the project or task may not be such a good idea. If my back feels happy as I think about a particular commitment I know it is okay to go ahead with it. When I am feeling overloaded and my back, neck and shoulders are starting to grumble then I know to offload something or take more rest before any serious pain sets in. Your health, whether good or bad, can be your friend.

When you are working hard on your goals and dreams, make a regular commitment to take time out and recharge yourself. In *The Artist's Way*, Julia Cameron suggests a weekly artist date. This is a date with yourself where you spend an hour or two doing something that nourishes you and replenishes your creative well. Ideas for artist dates may be going to see a film, taking time to browse in a favourite shop, visiting a gallery or exhibition, taking a walk at a local beauty spot or taking the time to sit somewhere that inspires you while enjoying your favourite beverage. Artist dates are an opportunity to do things that you never normally give yourself the time to do. They don't have to cost much money, in fact depending on what you want to do it might be free, and they don't have to take oodles of time. They should also be done alone. This is *your* time to replenish *yourself* according to *your* agenda and is not for the benefit of anyone else. Also, the artist date does not have to be directly connected to your dreams. For example, attending a seminar linked to your goals is not an artist date, it is a task from your action plan. Deciding to play hookey for an hour and wander through an antiques market enjoying checking out all the beautiful old furniture could be an artist date (unless of course your dream lies in the realm of antiques). When I go on an artist date I usually find that it inspires me to carry on with my dreams and sometimes gives me good ideas towards them. When I am worn out and feel that my work or writing is getting too hard or onerous, then I realise that I am probably overdue for an artist date. When I go on one I feel revived and ready to continue with my plans.

Exercise
What would you love to do for an artist date? Write down three ideas for potential dates. Now choose one of them and do it this week. If you find it to be fun, refreshing and inspiring then make plans for your next one.

Understanding how motivation works

We are either motivated in a 'towards' or 'away from' fashion. For example, if you want to earn money you may be motivated towards a specific sum or salary or professional achievement. Alternatively you may be motivated because you never want to be poor again or because you never want to have the experience of not being able to afford treats or buy essential clothing. Other examples of 'towards' motivation may be running a marathon because you want to attain a certain level of fitness or determining to be a best-selling author because you really feel that you have an important message to communicate to the world. An 'away from' motivation to running the marathon might be that you want to obliterate the experience of being the fat kid bringing up the rear of a race at school sports day. Similarly, an 'away from' drive for that best-selling book might be to get back at your English teacher at school who said that you would never amount to anything great.

'Towards' motivation is positive and based on a future achievement. 'Away from' motivation is negative and based on a past hurt. The purists in the personal development world would say that one should always find a 'towards' motivating factor when working towards a goal but I disagree. If a strong 'away from' motivation drives you forward to achieve great things then use it to your best advantage and construct something wonderful out of that previous painful experience.

Over time, you may find that an 'away from' motivation gradually changes to a 'towards' pattern. This happened to me with regards to my back. At first I did the exercises that the physiotherapist gave me to prevent another bad back but eventually I preferred to think of the exercises as being necessary for a happy and healthy back.

When you know what your motivating factor is then you can focus on that in tough times. It can help to regularly visualise yourself reaching your goal or to summon up how it might feel to satisfy your motivating factor.

Faith and prayer

As you already know, I practice Buddhism and I wish to state that this section is not about preaching the Buddhist message nor converting you to be a Buddhist. I do though wish to share my experiences of having a religion or living by a philosophical system. I believe that faith and prayer is a very effective way of bringing about deep seated change in yourself, understanding the nuances of your inner gremlin and having the courage to persist when the going gets tough.

If you were to ask me what I get from my Buddhist practice then my answer would be courage; the courage not to accept second best in my life. My practice gives me discipline and constant learning. I chant the Buddhist mantra every morning and evening and this gives structure to my day, to my goals and always gives me somewhere to go when I am frightened, daunted or angry at what lies ahead. Being a Buddhist doesn't make for an easy life. In fact I think it makes life more challenging because it doesn't allow me to sweep difficult areas of my life under the carpet.

My faith underpins everything that I do. It is the foundation on which everything else is based and as each year goes by that foundation gets stronger. I like to describe the feeling as having a strong iron column inside which allows my life to withstand whatever shows up in it. It may sway or bend slightly in the wind but it doesn't collapse. As the column gets stronger then it can withstand the weight of anything I need to hang from it. It is like having a spiritual backbone.

I am not prescribing that you must go forth and kindle a relationship with God, Jesus, Mohammed, Buddha or any other great sage. It is not my place to do that. But I will urge you to think about it. A couple of years ago I was at a talk given by Marianne Williamson, author of *Return To Love*. To be honest I can't remember much of what she said in the main body of the talk but I was very struck by her responses in the question and answer sessions that concluded the talk. There were three questions, all about difficult personal circumstances. The first was about caring for a sick relative, the second about lack of self confidence and the third about coping with the arrival of a new baby and how this added to time pressures in daily life. The first thing Marianne asked each person was did they have a regular practice of prayer and/or meditation. Each person replied that they meditated sometimes or had tried but it wasn't something that they did at the moment. Over the course of answering these three questions, Marianne explained that a daily practice of prayer and meditation allows one to have space for reflection, to buoy up one's life state before facing the pressures of the day and to gradually change negative tendencies and reaction into more considered ones. She advocated a prayer and meditative practice to support all facets of daily life. This is something that as a Buddhist I had been doing for over twenty years and it was good to hear someone else, a non-Buddhist, agree with me.

I remember once hearing a story about Gandhi where he was reflecting that he had an extremely busy day ahead of him so he had better do two hours of meditation rather than just one! In the busy lives that we lead today it can seem that we just don't have time to spend on daily religious or philosophical devotion. However, taking time for the daily prayer, determination and reflection can save us time. I know that the more I chant, the more I feel in rhythm with life. Work gets done quicker, my efforts are more focused and I seem to experience more synchronicity where I just happen to come across a person I need to meet or fall upon vital information. I have also witnessed in others the power of prayer and meditation to heal regrets. This has helped them move on from decisions made in the past that did not bring happiness and enabled them to start building new hope for the future.

If the idea of religion is totally unpalatable to you, that is okay. Instead I wonder if there is another activity that you can do 'religiously' that will give you the same benefit. For example, you may find benefit in going for a walk or a run in the morning before getting ready for work. Or you may like to keep a journal and regularly sifting through your thoughts and ascertain where you should focus your efforts for the day or next day. I have a friend who just doesn't feel right if she doesn't go swimming a couple of times a week. She swims religiously, she never lets anything get in the way of it and she says that it benefits her life enormously both physically and mentally. What can you do that will provide you with the discipline, structure and inspiration from which you can launch your dreams?

Your future revisited

Here we are at the end of the book. Leading the life you want to lead does not necessarily mean radical change. If you make just one degree of change in your attitude or action now, this small tangent as time progresses will take you to a different place than if you carry on exactly as you currently are.

Nothing is ever wasted on the journey to a fulfilled life. Even though your path may meander to some unexpected or unwelcome places, you will be surprised at how these may come in useful or be your saving grace in the future.

One of my favourite films is *It's A Wonderful Life*. I love to watch it every Christmas having first come across it a few years ago. For those of you who don't know this movie, it was made in 1946 by Frank Capra and stars Jimmy Stewart as George Bailey, a frustrated man living in a small town in America called Bedford

Falls. As a young man George had huge aspirations to travel the world, become an engineer and construct amazing buildings. However, one set of circumstances after another mean that George has to remain in Bedford Falls and grudgingly take over a small family run savings and loans association.

Last time I watched the film I was really struck by the pent-up rage that George feels and his resentment at being trapped in what he calls "a crummy little town". Over the years his peers and his brother get to leave the town and make something of themselves whereas George continues in his humble but valuable role of allowing the people of Bedford Falls to buy their own home.

The crux of the movie comes when, on Christmas Eve, a mistake causes George to have an $8,000 shortfall in the bank's accounts and he faces being carted off to prison. Clutching a $15,000 life assurance policy he realises that financially, he is worth more dead than alive.

George is saved when a guardian angel arrives and helps him to see how his life and his continual acts of kindness have made a hugely positive contribution to his friends, family and the town in general. He is finally convinced that the value of his life is far more than dollars, cents or glamorous achievement. In his hour of need the townspeople rally to help him and the film ends with his brother Harry declaring him the richest man in Bedford Falls.

Sometimes in our own hour of need we too can overlook our true worth and focus only on the negative or what we lack. At these times we need to remember our treasures of the heart – our capital in terms of friendship, love and humanity. Like George Bailey we can sometimes find it hard to grasp the positive contribution our life makes to our families, our places of work and our communities.

Please be assured that you have all the answers, resources and courage that you will ever need within you. It is just a case of drawing on them when you need them and having the courage to operate from your higher self or best potential. When you make the effort to be your best and do your best then the universe will respond to you. You will find the answers to your questions, the people that you need to help you will appear in your life and knowledge that you need to gain will present itself to you. You can lead the life you want to lead.

Exercise

For this final exercise, imagine that you have all the resources (time, money, knowledge, help) that you will ever need to achieve your dreams and imagine that all fear and procrastination has completely subsided. What are you free to go ahead and do now that you weren't before?

Next Steps

Thank you for buying this book. You can see more about my work and services at www.leadthelife.net and you can also read my blog. Additionally you can sign up for my newsletter. Every few weeks I send out food for thought articles and details of any talks or workshops that I am giving. I promise not to share your details with third parties and I won't bombard you with lots of emails.

You can also follow me on Twitter at
www.twitter.com/calibird.